S. HRG. 105–278

CONVEYANCE AND TRANSFER OF LANDS IN ALASKA

HEARING

BEFORE THE

COMMITTEE ON ENERGY AND NATURAL RESOURCES UNITED STATES SENATE

ONE HUNDRED FIFTH CONGRESS

FIRST SESSION

ON

S. 660

TO PROVIDE FOR THE CONTINUATION OF HIGHER EDUCATION THROUGH THE CONVEYANCE OF CERTAIN PUBLIC LANDS IN THE STATE OF ALASKA TO THE UNIVERSITY OF ALASKA, AND FOR OTHER PURPOSES

S. 1092

TO PROVIDE FOR A TRANSFER OF LAND INTERESTS TO FACILITATE SURFACE TRANSPORTATION BETWEEN THE CITIES OF COLD BAY, ALASKA, AND KING COVE, ALASKA, AND FOR OTHER PURPOSES

SEPTEMBER 11, 1997

Printed for the use of the
Committee on Energy and Natural Resources

U.S. GOVERNMENT PRINTING OFFICE

45–544 CC WASHINGTON : 1998

For sale by the U.S. Government Printing Office
Superintendent of Documents, Congressional Sales Office, Washington, DC 20402
ISBN 0-16-055975-8

COMMITTEE ON ENERGY AND NATURAL RESOURCES

CONTENTS

STATEMENTS

APPENDIX

CONVEYANCE AND TRANSFER OF LANDS IN ALASKA

THURSDAY, SEPTEMBER 11, 1997

U.S. SENATE,
COMMITTEE ON ENERGY AND NATURAL RESOURCES,
Washington, DC.

The committee met, pursuant to notice, at 9:33 a.m., in room SD–366, Dirksen Senate Office Building, Hon. Frank Murkowski, chairman, presiding.

OPENING STATEMENT OF HON. FRANK H. MURKOWSKI, U.S. SENATOR FROM ALASKA

The CHAIRMAN. Good morning. We will call the hearing of the Energy and Natural Resources Committee to order. We again are faced with objections from the minority relative to the hearing process today and I am not sure just how long we are going to be able to go. Unfortunately, this is an issue that involves a procedure, and once an objection is initiated there is really not much that a chairman can do about it other than apologize to those witnesses that are coming.

So I intend to try and get as much on the record as possible in the time that we have. We have four stacked votes beginning at 10 o'clock and as a consequence the limitation for the hearing on the minimum would be to terminate the hearing at approximately 11:30. But as a consequence of the circumstances, I am going to be asking Brian Malnak and/or Gregg Renkes continue to proceed with the agenda during my absence when I am voting. So I assume there is no particular objection to that, and if there is we are going to do it anyway.

I am going to start with the Alaska witnesses and not the Government people this morning. So you folks can relax back there. Some of you are familiar with your seats. What we are going to do is we are going to call the group from King Cove up first and that will initiate testimony from: Mr. Gary Hennigh, city manager, city of King Cove; Jack Hession, Sierra Club; Marvin Hoff, president of the Agdaagux Tribal Council; and Della Trumble, secretary-treasurer, the King Cove Corporation.

As they come up, I will proceed with a very brief statement with regard to the availability of a road from King Cove to Cold Bay. I think this legislation, S. 1092, provides a balanced approach to a very difficult problem. This bill would permit King Cove to be connected to the rest of the world through a road link to Cold Bay, the location of a good all-weather airport which exists at Cold Bay, which can provide emergency medical evacuation for the residents of King Cove.

In exchange for providing the easement, the Federal Government gets fee simple title to some of King Cove's land that the Fish and Wildlife previously stated they wanted.

Since 1981—and I think my friend from Colorado would appreciate this—there have been 11 air crash fatalities that have occurred flying residents from King Cove to Cold Bay. Numerous other crashes have also occurred, luckily without fatalities. Most of these crashes involved med-evac flights. Often the trip to care in King Cove is as dangerous as the affliction itself. With no road link, there is no hope for those seeking help.

This bill provides for an exchange that will allow a short road to be built by King Cove and Cold Bay. I understand the concerns about the impact on the Izembek National Wildlife Refuge and it is not my intent to belittle that by any means. I have been out there. I have traveled the area. I know the road system. I know the roads that are already in the wilderness.

During a former debate on access in this body, the administration and my friends on the committee have said from time to time: Well, just show me where you need specific access across Federal areas and why you need that access and we will help you get that access if it is legitimate. Well, here is their perfect opportunity. And I think there is a case for R.S. 2477 based on traditional trapping and foot traffic in the area, which I understand that there is a map before the committee that indicates the traditional use of footpaths for trapping over an extended period of time.

There is simply no alternative to this except further danger to our constituents and the inevitability of harm to future victims in the next air crash. I stand ready to work with the Fish and Wildlife Service to make this as constructive a process as possible. But make no mistake, the King Cove residents in my opinion deserve a way to save themselves from the emergencies associated with operating in and out of King Cove in the winter time, when at one end of the runway the wind sock will be blowing one way and on the other end it will be blowing the other way. This is not an exaggeration.

I do not think we can continue to let these residents be hostage to fear for life and limb.

[The prepared statement of Senator Murkowski follows:]

Prepared Statement of Hon. Frank H. Murkowski, U.S. Senator From Alaska

Good morning. Today we will hear testimony on S. 660, the University of Alaska land grant legislation, and S. 1092, providing for surface transportation between King Cove, Alaska and Cold Bay, Alaska.

S. 660 (UNIVERSITY)

The University of Alaska (University) is the only land grant college in the country without land. S. 660 puts the University on equal footing with other land grant institutions. It provides the University with the land needed to support itself financially and continue to act as a responsible steward of the land and educator of our children.

Specifically, S. 660 would grant the University 250,000 acres of federal land. The University would then be eligible to receive an additional 250k federal acres on a matching basis with the state for a total of 500k additional acres.

Under this legislation there are significant restrictions on the land the University can select. The University cannot select land that is located within a conservation system unit, that is validly conveyed to the state or an ANCSA corporation, or land that is used in connection with federal or military institutions. Additionally, under this legislation the University must relinquish its inholdings in Alaska once it receives its selection awarded under this bill.

These inholdings include the Alaska Peninsula and Maritime National Wildlife Refuge, the Kenai Fjords National Park, Wrangell-St. Elias National Park and Preserve, and Denali Park and Preserve.

S. 660 allows the state to participate in the process as well on an optional basis. No action on behalf of the state is directed by this legislation!

I am disappointed the state is not here to testify. In their absence, I want to clarify some issues the state has confused about this legislation. First, the Governor has stated "your bill specifically identifies transfer of National Petroleum Reserve-Alaska and Tongass National Forest lands." This is simply untrue. Nowhere in this bill are those lands specifically identified. Second, the Governor has stated he is opposed to any state match requirement stating this bill will "put the federal government's hands on the steering wheel of state decision making." This is also untrue. In fact, under this legislation, the opposite is true and if the state chooses to grant the University additional lands the federal government must also do so. Furthermore, the legislature currently can, and has, passed legislation transferring lands to the University. This legislation does not change that in any way.

Many people feel the state, because of large land grant under the Statehood, should be responsible for the University's land grant. I remind people that currently this is the picture of land ownership in Alaska:

Total land mass—365 million acres
State lands—104 million acres
Native lands—44 million acres
Federal lands—248 million acres
- NPS lands—54 million acres
- FWS lands—76 million acres
- BLM lands—90 million acres
- Wilderness—57 million acres

The fact is that the University is a federal land grant university and has received less federal land than almost any other land grant college in the continental U.S.

With the passage of this bill, the University of Alaska will finally be able to act fully as a land grant college. It will be able to select lands that can provide the University with a stable income as well as provide responsible stewardship for the land.

I look forward to hearing from witnesses and seeing S. 660 enacted into law.

S. 1092 (KING COVE ROAD)

S. 1092, provides a balanced approach to a difficult problem. S. 1092 will permit King Cove to be connected to the rest of the world through a road link to Cold Bay, the location of a good, all-weather airport which can provide emergency medical evacuation for the residents of King Cove.

In exchange for providing the easement, the federal government gets fee simple title to some King Cove lands, lands the FWS has previously stated they want.

Since 1981, eleven (11) air crash fatalities have occurred flying residents from King Cove to Cold Bay. Numerous other crashes also have occurred, luckily without fatalities. Many of these crashes involved medivac flights where often the trip to care in King Cove is as dangerous as the infliction itself.

With no road link there is no hope for those seeking help. This bill provides for an exchange that will allow a short road to be built between King Cove and Cold Bay. I understand concerns about the impact on the Izembek National Wildlife Refuge and do not want to belittle these. However, currently there exits some 47 miles of road in the King Cove/Cold Bay area. Approximately 10 to 15 miles currently are in the wilderness portion of these lands which I understand have been used to some degree for the past 17 years. A maximum of 7 miles of new road across federal lands are needed.

During former debates on access in this body, the Administration and my friends on this Committee have said, "show me where you need specific access and why and we will help." Here is the perfect opportunity! There is no alternative to this except further danger to my constituents and the inevitable harm to future victims of the next air crash.

I stand ready to work with the Fish and Wildlife Service to make this as constructive a process as possible; but make no mistake, the King Cove residents deserve a way to save their lives in times of emergency. They cannot be hostage to fear for life and limb.

I look forward to hearing from our witnesses today.

The CHAIRMAN. Senator Campbell, do you have any comments?

Senator CAMPBELL. No opening statement, Mr. Chairman.

The CHAIRMAN. All right, I appreciate that.

I would ask the witnesses from King Cove to proceed as they see fit.

STATEMENT OF GARY HENNIGH, CITY MANAGER, KING COVE, ALASKA, ACCOMPANIED BY STEVE SILVER, COUNSEL, ALEUTIANS EAST BOROUGH, ALASKA

Mr. HENNIGH. Thank you, Mr. Chairman.

My name is Gary Hennigh. The mayor of the city of King Cove, Arthur Newman, was originally scheduled to testify today on behalf of King Cove, but was unable to attend because of the fishing season. Mayor Newman is a commercial fisherman and, as the chairman knows, the 1997 salmon season has again been a disaster for us. The region, however, is experiencing an unanticipated late run of silver salmon, and the Mayor felt compelled to stay with his setnet site in order that his family might eat this winter. He has asked me to present his testimony for the record in support of S. 1092.

Accompanying me today on the left is Mr. Steve Silver, counsel for the Aleutians East Borough. Mr. Silver is prepared to respond to any questions you may have relating to our position on legal issues related to S.1092, as well as to point out certain key features on the graphics that we have with us.

I would like to draw your attention to several key issues related to safe access to and from King Cove, Alaska. We do not have reliable and safe access to medical facilities like most Americans. The response to medical emergencies are constantly hampered by the lack of reliable transportation. In 1980, a crab fisherman lost his foot in an accident and the med-evac plane delivering him to Cold Bay crashed, killing all four people aboard. Since that crash, another seven people have been killed flying between King Cove and Cold Bay in small planes.

A few years ago, because of poor flying and boating conditions, a heart attack victim had to wait 3 days before he could be medevacced out. When every minute counts, we are 625 air miles from the nearest hospital in Anchorage, and we cannot even deliver our loved ones to the Cold Bay Airport to begin the life or death journey. Because we live in a close-knit community where many of us are related to each other, we all are traumatized when someone dies or suffers needlessly when we cannot get them to medical care.

We do not have reliable and safe transportation accessibility to and from our community, which most Americans simply take for granted. Flying into King Cove in a small plane can be a terrifying experience, and this is not due to a deficient airstrip. Either severe wind conditions or fog, complicated by steep, mountainous terrain, makes the flight to and from Cold Bay, which is our major destination to access other places in Alaska, to be 10 minutes of anxiety much of the time.

The CHAIRMAN. I wonder if you could put—I think you have got some pictures of our airstrip, do you not? Go ahead and proceed. I just think it would be beneficial.

Mr. HENNIGH. Residents have had such horrific flights that an intense fear of flying is a common phobia amongst the residents of King Cove. This fear causes residents to severely restrict their activities. For example, we have qualified candidates for the school board, borough assembly, and city council seats who decline to serve because serving requires flying in and out of King Cove for meetings and trainings.

The graphic that is being put on the easel at the moment shows the mountainous terrain——

The CHAIRMAN. We have got another easel over here. Why do you not use both of them.

All right, go ahead.

Mr. HENNIGH. I will come back to those in just a second.

Improvements in aviation infrastructure do not solve this basic problem. It would require the Federal Government to remove several mountains in order to expand the King Cove airstrip and provide a crosswind runway for small aircraft. Even if improvements are made to the takeoff and landings at King Cove, there have been numerous incidents in the past where the small med-evac planes have crashed trying to land in Cold Bay, which has a world class runway and crosswind runway. Small planes simply cannot handle the flying conditions during certain weather conditions in the region.

This particular graphic was taken on one of the few days in King Cove when you have blue sky and you have a view of the volcanic mountains surrounding you, the airstrip in the middle. You fly to the body of water called Leonard Harbor to start the 7 to 10-minutes of terrifying flight to get over to Cold Bay under most normal circumstances.

The CHAIRMAN. So the wind comes off either side of the mountains and your runway is up and down in the gut, is that right?

Mr. HENNIGH. Yes, sir, Mr. Chairman. And as you mentioned, we can have the wind sock at one end of the runway blowing to the north and the wind sock at the other end of the runway blowing to the south, depending upon which direction the prevailing winds are coming at any given moment.

Transportation by boat is not reliable either because often the same poor weather conditions make boating an impossible or treacherous endeavor. When we have been able to med-evac patients to Cold Bay by sea, we have been confronted with the dangerous offloading conditions at the Cold Bay dock. The injured, the sick and the elderly occasionally have to be offloaded using a sling or a rope pulley system which is precarious in the best of conditions and downright difficult when buffeted by high winds.

The seas in Cold Bay can be just as violent during the winter storms as anywhere else in the Gulf of Alaska or the Bering Sea. Even if we had a safe place to dock a boat in Cold Bay, where there is no current wave barrier, we are asking fishermen to risk their lives and their commercial fishing vessels in attempting to make the crossing to Cold Bay during heavy seas.

The construction of a bridge is not feasible because of the distance between the closest points of land. A bridge might physically work to link the two communities, provided that the Federal Government wants to make an investment in an asset that would be longer than the Chesapeake Bay Bridge in order to link a village of 900 people with a community of 150 people. We just do not believe that this fiscally prudent Congress intends to pursue an option that is likely to cost $100 million to build.

Road access through the refuge to Cold Bay is the only reliable and safe alternative for the residents of King Cove. We are only 19 road miles away from one of the biggest and best airports and Alaska. The severe weather, high winds, rain, snow, fog which make small aircraft flying or boating a questionable mode of transportation does not have the same effect on a road. From our experience, a road is the only safe and cost efficient answer.

Additional testimony has been provided to support statements made in this testimony today, as well as a critique of the Fish and Wildlife Service's briefing paper on this subject. We believe that that particular briefing paper has some serious inaccuracies that we have pointed out.

In conclusion, the city of King Cove is requesting your support for getting the necessary easement through the Izembek National Wildlife Refuge. I am confident that the type of road we envision can be constructed in an environmentally balanced manner. We humans and the wildlife and the waterfowl that use the Izembek Refuge and adjacent areas can survive in harmony with the road just the same as we have without a road.

Thank you, Mr. Chairman.

[The prepared statement of Mr. Hennigh follows:]

PREPARED STATEMENT OF GARY HENNIGH, CITY MANAGER, KING COVE, AK

My name is Gary Hennigh. The Mayor of the City of King Cove, Arthur Newman, was originally scheduled to testify today on behalf of King Cove but was unable to attend because of the fishing season. Mayor Newman is a commercial fisherman and, as the Chairman knows, the 1997 season has been a disaster. The Region is experiencing an unanticipated late run of silver salmon, and the Mayor felt compelled to stay with his set net sight in order that his family might eat this winter. He has asked me to present his testimony for the record in support of S. 1092. Accompanying me today is Mr. Steve Silver, counsel for the Aleutians East Borough. Mr. Silver is prepared to respond to any questions you may have relating to our position on legal issues related to S. 1092.

I would like to draw your attention to several key issues related to safe access to and from King Cove.

We do not have reliable and safe access to medical facilities like most Americans. The response to medical emergencies are hampered by lack of reliable transportation. In 1980, a crab fisherman lost his foot in an accident and the medivac delivering him to Cold Bay crashed killing all four aboard. Several years ago, because of poor flying and boating conditions, a heart attack victim had to wait three days to be medivaced out. When every minute counts, we are 625 air miles from the nearest hospital in Anchorage and we can't even deliver our loved ones to Cold Bay airport to begin the life or death journey. Because we live in a close knit community, where many of us are related to each other, we all are traumatized when someone dies or suffers needlessly when we can't get them to medical care.

We do not have reliable and safe transportation accessibility to and from our community, which most Americans take for granted. Flying into King Cove in a small plane can be a terrifying experience. This is not due to a deficient airstrip. Either severe wind conditions or fog, complicated by steep, mountainous terrain, makes the flight to/from Cold Bay (our major destination to access other transportation options) to be ten minutes of anxiety much of the time. Residents have had such horrific flights that an intense fear of flying is a common phobia. This fear causes residents to severely restrict their activities. For example, we have qualified potential candidates for school board, Borough Assembly and City Council seats who decline to serve because serving requires flying in and out of King Cove for meetings and training.

Improvements in aviation infrastructure don't solve this basic problem. It would require the Federal Government to remove several mountains in order to expand the King Cove air strip and provide a cross-wind runway for small aircraft. Even if improvements are made to take off and land at King Cove, there have been incidents in the past where the small medivac planes have crashed trying to land in Cold Bay, which has a world-class runway and cross runway. Small planes simply cannot handle flying conditions during certain weather conditions in the region.

Transportation by boat is not reliable because oftentimes the same poor weather conditions make boating an impossible or treacherous endeavor. When we have been able to medivac patients to Cold Bay by sea, we have been confronted with dangerous off-loading conditions at the Cold Bay dock. The injured, sick and elderly occasionally have to be off-loaded using a sling or rope pulley system which is precarious in the best of conditions and downright difficult when buffeted by high winds. The seas in Cold Bay can be just as violent during the winter storms as anywhere else in the Gulf of Alaska or the Bering Sea. Even if we had a safe place to dock a boat in Cold Bay (where no wave barrier protection currently exists), we are asking fishermen to risk their lives and their commercial fishing vessels in attempting to make the crossing to Cold Bay during heavy sea states.

The construction of a bridge is not feasible because of the distance between the closest points of land. A bridge might physically work to link the two communities, provided that the Federal Government wants to make an investment in an asset that would be longer than the Chesapeake Bay Bridge, in order to link a village of 1,000 people with a community of 150 people. We just don't believe that this fiscally prudent Congress intends to pursue an option that is likely to cost $100 million, and be too costly to maintain.

Road access through the Refuge to Cold Bay is the only reliable and safe alternative for the residents of King Cove. We are only nineteen (proposed) road miles away from one of the biggest and best airports in Alaska. The severe weather (high winds, rain, snow, fog) which make small aircraft flying or boating a questionable mode of transportation does not have the same effect on a road. From our experience, a road is the only safe and cost-efficient answer.

Also attached to this testimony are comments provided by staff of the Aleutians East Borough which critique the Fish and Wildlife Service's briefing paper on this subject. We feel that the Service portrayal of the road is inaccurate.

In conclusion, the City of King Cove is requesting your support for getting the necessary easement through the Izembek National Wildlife Refuge. I am confident that the type of road we envision can be constructed in an environmentally-balanced and easily enforceable manner. We humans, and the wildlife and water fowl that use the Izembek Refuge and adjacent areas, can survive in harmony with a road just the same as we have without the road.

Notes on USES Briefing Statement (March 13, 1997) on the King Cove-Cold Buy Road Project Through Part of the Izembek National Wildlife Refuge

In general, the USFWS briefing statement simply makes assertions of potential and "probable" impact rather than explaining and proving how such impacts would occur. They list a number of unique values of the Izembek NWR, but these descriptions (such as habitat values for Pacific brant, Steller's eiders, the SAP caribou herd, brown bears, and other animals) generally apply to the Refuge as a whole (i.e., over 300,000 acres), not to the proposed road corridor itself.

Moreover, the briefing statement makes assertions, without backup, about drainage and pollution impacts and potential effects of increased access of the proposed road, without acknowledging that existing roads and the town and airport of Cold Bay anchor one end of the proposed road corridor and make any such incremental effects of the proposed road minuscule.

Some particulars

In 1985, the King Cove Road project was not just identified in the Bristol Bay Management Plan, it was included in the preferred alternative.

The Refuge's negative response at the time, in the *Izembek National Wildlife Refuge (NWR) Comprehensive Conservation Plan (CCP)*, was no better than that in this briefing: they asserted rather than demonstrated potential impacts. Most notably, they asserted that the road would improve access into sensitive brown bear habitat in the Joshua Green River and Left and Right hand Valleys (CCP at page 118), yet they failed to state that there would still be more than five miles of separation through which no motorized traffic would be allowed—and that those areas already support the vast majority of recreational brown bear hunting, thus are already "disturbed" (CCP at page 84, fig. 24.).

The USFWS also asserts that the road would impact the local South Alaska Peninsula caribou herd. Yet, in their Comprehensive Conservation Plan (CCP at page 57, fig. 18) they show that the area of the proposed road corridor is not key habitat (but the existing road from Cold Bay to Grant Point is in such key habitat). It seems a bit disingenuous for the USFWS to assert that the proposed road, which parallels the "Kinzarof Isthmus,' is now considered a hazard to caribou migration, while the existing road to Grant Point, which cuts directly across that isthmus and accommodates refuge-sponsored traffic to a viewing station on the shore of Izembek Lagoon, is not mentioned as such a hazard. Is there really much hazard?

The USFWS also cites possible effects of sedimentation from road-building and traffic into local drainages as possible impacts to Kinzarof and Izembek Lagoons. Yet, this area is notably flat, with very few connecting drainages. It is close to none of the drainages mentioned in the Water Resources section of the Izembek Refuge CCP (at page 32, which specifically mentions the distant Joshua Green River and drainages off Frosty Peak to Izembek Lagoon). Moreover, according to the CCP vegetation maps, the proposed road corridor is considered "open low shrub graminoid" rather than "wet bog/wet meadow," thus further indicating the corridor's relative dryness and lesser susceptibility to flooding, erosion, and transport of pollutants than other areas of the refuge.

Regarding waterfowl, other than tundra swans, they mostly occur and utilize the lagoon systems themselves which would not be crossed, nor directly accessed, by the proposed road (in contrast to direct access to Izembek Lagoon provided by the existing Grant Point and Outer Marker roads). It is unlikely that brant rafting in the extensive lagoon eelgrass beds would notice, let alone negatively respond to, traffic on a proposed road on the uplands.

Finally, the Izembek Refuge does appear to have a relatively unique population of resident tundra swans (although they mostly winter on Unimak Island). Yet, even according to the map of tundra swan distribution provided with the March 13, 1997 briefing paper, the proposed road corridor does a pretty good job of skirting any important breeding and molting areas in the refuge.

Back to generalities

In the briefing, the USFWS makes a number of assertions but does not provide any demonstration of impacts. And, they make a number of overly strong statements, for example:

On briefing page 3, they state they "have grave concerns for any proposal to construct a road through the Kinzarof Isthmus". Aside from not giving any real indication about the "gravity", it is interesting to note that the term "Kinzarof Isthmus" and its newly alleged importance does not even appear in previous documents like the Comprehensive Conservation Plan. In *Part II—Special Values of Izembek Refuge* (CCP at page 14) there is a list of the agency's identified "special values" for the refuge: they include a number of places but specifically not the "Kinzarof Isthmus" nor the area encompassed by the road corridor.

On briefing page 6, they state that vehicle traffic and other presumed impacts of the proposed road "would degrade the wildland experience of refuge users throughout much of the northern portion of the Izembek Wilderness." Yet, a quick look at their map would show that most of that northern portion includes the Joshua Green River drainage and areas further distant from the road—areas not likely to be effected at all by access, noise, or even visual disturbance from the road corridor.

On briefing page 6, they also state that road construction "would probably result in increased silt load or decreased fresh-water flowing into Kinzarof Lagoon . . ." First of all, they provide no indication why such an impact is probable; second, flat relatively dry tundra is not a uniquely difficult area upon which to construct a road with adequate drainage through it.

On briefing page 7, they state that brant are sensitive to "disturbance levels which would be elevated if the proposed road was constructed." Again, this is an assertion with no identifiable basis. Moreover, the brant are typically well out into the lagoon systems, not on the uplands nor proposed road corridor. There is currently little impact attributed to disturbance of brant from the existing road to Grant Point, which proceeds directly to the edge of the lagoon and brant resting areas, so why is it natural to presume that the more-upland proposed road would result in such disturbance?

A parting shot

Appendix A to the *Record of Decision for the Izembek National Wildlife Refuge (NWR) Comprehensive Conservation Plan (CCP)*, dated 1985, states clearly the USFWS's understanding that Congressional approval is required to build the road across the refuge. It seems a bit disingenuous, again, that the Service has put this effort off for a year under the guise of working out some other method outside the Congressional arena and now seems surprised that advocates are again going to Congress for an appropriate easement.

The CHAIRMAN. Thank you very much. I appreciate your testimony, Gary.

Our next witness from King Cove, Mr. Marvin Hoff, president of the Tribal Council. Good morning.

STATEMENT OF MARVIN HOFF, PRESIDENT, AGDAAGUX TRIBAL COUNCIL, ANCHORAGE, AK

Mr. HOFF. Good morning. Mr. Chairman, my name is Marvin Hoff. I am here on behalf of myself. I am a 53-year resident of King Cove. I am also the president of the Agdaagux Tribal Council, which has a membership of about 613 Aleuts.

The CHAIRMAN. Speak a little louder, would you, please. A little closer to the mike would help, if you would just move the mike over. Thank you.

Mr. HOFF. I am very much in favor of a road between King Cove and Cold Bay. If we had such a road, my first wife Cathy would be alive today. She was a licensed practical nurse escorting an injured fisherman out of King Cove to Anchorage via Cold Bay. They were on a med-evac plane and the flying weather was bad. It was a life or death situation for the fisherman and Cathy felt she had to go with him. The plane crashed shortly after taking off from the King Cove airstrip.

We have frequent med-evac situations in King Cove in poor weather conditions, and I hold my breath each time, fearing a repeat of this disaster.

Our safety problem is real. We live with it every day. I am here to ask the Congress to give us a road so people in our community have a safe way of leaving King Cove, especially in emergencies.

While I am here I would also like to comment on the King Cove road briefing report written by the Fish and Wildlife Service in May 1997. I would like to correct some inaccurate information presented in the Service's report so members of Congress have the benefit of local experience with the wildlife resources of the Izembek Refuge.

The report identifies this as a pristine wilderness area. The area in fact has many roads, including one that already goes behind most of Kinzarof Lagoon. The Service has tried to cut off these roads by prohibiting access beyond certain points on the old road system. All of these roads are used intensely by hunters from around the world. Whole planeloads, hundreds of people at a time, fly into Cold Bay to hunt this area. They all use the existing roads that were put in during World War II.

Many of the locals also use their boats to subsistence hunt and fish along the shoreline of the refuge, exactly where the road would be located.

The report raises concerns about hunting along the proposed corridor. An aerial survey of the caribou population was done by the

Service in coordination with local residents from King Cove, Cold Bay, Falls Pass, and Nelson's Lagoon. This survey showed 50 percent of the caribou, 1,500 to 2,000 animals, winter along the road system. During the years when the caribou herd was at its highest, hundreds of trophy hunters flew into Cold Bay for a road hunt on all the existing roads within the refuge.

The road is not going to change the subsistence hunting and fishing because we already take what we need by boat. The feds can regulate non-subsistence hunts within the refuge whether there is a road or not. Out of State hunters can harvest our caribou and other wildlife on the many miles of road within the region, but the locals are deprived of a gravel road along the coast to protect their families in King Cove. The position of the feds does not make much sense to us.

The report also states the Pacific brant use Kinzarof Lagoon during the winter. They do not use Kinzarof Lagoon in winter, but overwinter in Hook Bay or Snack Island outside the proposed road corridor.

I believe the estimates for Emperor geese at 55,000 were closer to 80,000 in 1996, and I have never seen 5,000 to 8,000 Emperors in these lagoons during the winter months.

Steller's eiders do not molt and overwinter in these lagoons, as the Service reports. Steller's molt and nest in the Arctic. Neither I nor anyone else in the region have ever seen Steller's in these lagoons during the winter or summer months. They are instead seen throughout the Alaska peninsula, primarily at sea.

Tundra swan do not winter in the Kinzarof Lagoon or Izembek area. They molt and nest in the many lakes around the existing Cold Bay road system and throughout the Alaska peninsula.

I believe that the Service is underestimating the caribou population. The population is at 3500 to 4,000 animals, roughly twice the Service's estimate.

The brown bear population has also been underestimated in the report and has actually increased in the past 5 years all over the peninsula.

In closing, I urge you to take into consideration the points that I have made and can justify with local knowledge and experience. We deserve to have safe transportation to and from our home, just like other Americans. I also think it is important for Congress to have the most accurate information about the natural resources of Izembek Refuge. The lifetime experience of people who live in the region should be valued in your decisionmaking process.

Thank you for the opportunity to speak to you today.

The CHAIRMAN. Thank you very much, Mr. Hoff.

Ms. Trumble, secretary-treasurer, King Cove Corporation. Good morning.

STATEMENT OF DELLA TRUMBLE, SECRETARY-TREASURER, KING COVE CORPORATION, ANCHORAGE, AK

Ms. TRUMBLE. Mr. Chairman, my name is Della Trumble. I am the secretary-treasurer for the King Cove Corporation in King Cove, Alaska. Our corporation is a village corporation as defined by the Alaska Native Claims Settlement Act. Our shareholders are of Aleut descent, whose ancestors have lived in and around the King

Cove region for thousands of years. I have been with the corporation for 21 years, as a director and officer for 19 of those years and an employee for 21 years.

The King Cove Corporation owns the majority of the land in the city of King Cove and the city of Cold Bay. We have lands within the Izembek National Wildlife Refuge that are subject to section 22(g) of ANCSA. Our land includes most of the coast of Cold Bay, and I mean the bay itself when I make this statement. We have this land outlined on a large map and we can point it out for you if you wish.

The CHAIRMAN. Go ahead.

Ms. TRUMBLE. Steve will——

The CHAIRMAN. Well, you are going to have to speak because the recorder——

Ms. TRUMBLE. I cannot see the map from where I am.

The CHAIRMAN. Well, we obviously did not rehearse this.

Ms. TRUMBLE. Basically, what we are looking at, there is an existing 5 miles of road to the existing airport in King Cove. We are looking at approximately another 7 miles from that road to the land that starts, our lands that are subject to 22(g) in the wilderness refuge. 7 miles of that land is our land. The other 7 miles is the easement that we are asking for.

The CHAIRMAN. And that would be an easement across the wilderness?

Ms. TRUMBLE. Yes.

The CHAIRMAN. Are there any other roads in that wilderness?

Ms. TRUMBLE. Yes, there are existing roads. The white line there is an existing road. That probably has been shortened over the years with wildlife management.

The CHAIRMAN. How many miles is that road?

Ms. TRUMBLE. Probably about 5 miles.

The CHAIRMAN. 5 miles of road in the wilderness now?

Ms. TRUMBLE. Yes.

The CHAIRMAN. Thank you.

Ms. TRUMBLE. There are also existing roads that head up northerly and the refuge, for approximately probably a total of maybe 22 or 25 miles.

The CHAIRMAN. That are in the refuge?

Ms. TRUMBLE. That are in the refuge at this time.

The CHAIRMAN. But are not in the wilderness? I am trying to distinguish between the two.

Ms. TRUMBLE. Can Steve help me? I am having a hard time with this.

Mr. SILVER. Mr. Chairman, we estimate that there is about 10 to 15 miles of road, preexisting road built by the military during World War Two, but used essentially up to the present day, subject to Fish and Wildlife Service regulation, inside the wilderness. It is this road that extends up to Strawberry Point, which is at the end of the wilderness. And there is also a road that goes back here.

The CHAIRMAN. Thank you. Please proceed.

Ms. TRUMBLE. Section 22(g) of ANCSA puts a restriction on the use of our land. It says that we can only use it in a manner consistent with the purposes of the refuge. Our land within the refuge falls within a wilderness designation.

The corporation has been an active and vocal proponent of the road for years. This is, above all, a safety issue. We strongly support a safer mode of travel between the two communities. We do not want anyone else to be killed in trying to get to King Cove, from King Cove to Cold Bay, or to continue increasing the risks of medical complications of injured or sick people when they cannot get out of King Cove for several days at a time.

This is so important to the corporation, its shareholders, their children, and the other residents of King Cove that we are willing to give up land in exchange solely for an easement to build the road.

We have tried on a number of occasions to convince the Fish and Wildlife Service to enter into a land exchange that would permit the road. The first proposal was made in 1986. In 1995, we again offered a possible acre for acre land exchange for wetlands in the Martinson's Lagoon area. Our vice president at the time, Kenneth Mack, met with the Service staff in Anchorage to discuss the land exchange and was told that the only way we could possibly get access is by congressional action because the Service would not grant a road easement through a wilderness area.

We made another proposal again this year. The present proposal was not an actual acre for acre trade, but would instead involve an exchange of lands for an easement through the refuge. The lands we offered are on the outside of Kinzarof Lagoon and the Service recognizes that there is high habitat value. We were nonetheless turned down on this offer.

The offer is reflected in the terms of H.R. 2259. If you would like, we can show you where the land is on this map.

The CHAIRMAN. Go ahead.

Ms. TRUMBLE. We need an easement for the entire road within Izembek. The majority of the road would run across the corporations 22(g) lands. The remainder, about 6 to 7 miles, runs through a wilderness area which is owned by the Federal Government.

We are willing to give up fee simple title to our lands described in the legislation in return for a legislated easement for the road. All we want is safe access for our people. We see the road as our only hope.

Thank you, Mr. Chairman.

The CHAIRMAN. Thank you very much.

Mr. Hession, good morning. Nice to see you here again. Please proceed.

STATEMENT OF JACK HESSION, ALASKA REPRESENTATIVE, THE SIERRA CLUB, ANCHORAGE, AK

Mr. HESSION. Good morning, Mr. Chairman. Thank you for this opportunity to present our views.

If I may submit my full statement for the record, I will briefly summarize it.

The CHAIRMAN. Without objection.

Mr. HESSION. Thank you.

The CHAIRMAN. A little hard to hear you this morning, Jack. So why do you not pull up your microphone.

Mr. HESSION. Mr. Chairman, we fully support improved transportation between King Cove and Cold Bay and note that there are a number of ways to achieve this worthy goal. But we strongly oppose S. 1092 because its preferred alternative, a road across Izembek National Wildlife Refuge, would have severe adverse consequences to refuge wildlife and habitats, as shown by the U.S. Fish and Wildlife Service's analysis.

At this point may I ask that this analysis be introduced into the record.

The CHAIRMAN. Yes. Would you give a description of what it says?

Mr. HESSION. It is the August 1997 King Cove road briefing report by the U.S. Fish and Wildlife Service.

The CHAIRMAN. Without objection, it is entered into the record.*

Mr. HESSION. Thank you.

Izembek National Wildlife Refuge and Izembek State Wildlife Refuge is one of the State's, the Nation's, and the world's most important protected fish and wildlife areas. From the Federal side, of course, it is almost entirely protected as a unit of the National Wilderness Preservation System.

Currently the State Department of Transportation and Public Facilities has under way an intermodal transportation project that is considering improved transportation to the lower Alaska peninsula, and with respect to the King Cove-Cold Bay road it is currently looking at six ways of improving transportation between these two communities. One is continued reliance on existing air service and private vessels. The second is the proposed King Cove-Cold Bay road. The third is a new airport for King Cove; fourth, a new regular ferry service linking the two communities; fifth, hovercraft service; and sixth, a med-evac helicopter serving communities on the lower Alaska peninsula—King Cove, Cold Bay, Fall's Pass, Port Moller, and perhaps others.

The last two alternatives address the need for improved med-evac service. The other three that I mentioned—road, airport, and ferry—would also further economic and community development objectives.

Mr. Chairman, although the study is under way, as I mentioned, preliminary analysis indicates that a new ferry system link can offer safer and more reliable service than the proposed road. In the ranking done by the Department, there was an insignificant difference in feasibility between the two modes.

At this point, sir, I ask that the Department of Transportation's preliminary analysis entitled "King Cove-Cold Bay Access, Reconnaissance Study Report of October 1994" be included in the record.

The CHAIRMAN. It will be entered in the record.

Mr. HESSION. Thank you, sir.

In summary, Mr. Chairman, we recommend that the committee take no further action on S. 1092, instead await the results of the transportation planning process. This process is making good progress in addressing the transportation needs of King Cove and Cold Bay, as well as other communities on the lower Alaska peninsula.

Thank you very much, sir.

[The prepared statement of Mr. Hession follows:]

---

*The report has been retained in committee files.

Prepared Statement of Jack Hession, Alaska Representative, the Sierra Club, Anchorage, AK

Good morning. My name is Jack Hession. I am the Alaska Representative of the Sierra Club, which is a national environmental organization of about 650,000 members with chapters in every state. I live in Anchorage, Alaska.

In summary, although the Sierra Club fully supports improved transportation between King Cove and Cold Bay for improved safety and other reasons, we cannot support the road alternative that would be facilitated by enactment of this bill.

S. 1092 would create a road right-of-way (ROW) across Izembek Wilderness in the Izembek National Wildlife Refuge. Should a road then be constructed within this ROW, the likely adverse impacts on the refuge and the wilderness would be severe. Hence, we strongly oppose this bill, and urge the selection through the State's transportation process, now underway, of an appropriate alternative.

S. 1092 and the Izembek Wilderness

S. 1092 would grant to the Aleutians East Borough a 100-foot-wide ROW across 11 miles of the Izembek National Wildlife Refuge, including 7 miles of Izembek Wilderness, provided that the King Cove (Native) corporation first conveyed 1,920 acres of its own land to the federal government for addition to the refuge. This borough-owned ROW would facilitate the construction of a road linking Cold Bay with King Cove. Since the corporation is a proponent of a road, the conveyance of the necessary acreage is assured.

S. 1092 imposes this ROW regardless of the environmental impact on refuge resources and wilderness values of a subsequent road. These resources and values are nicely summarized, and the likely environmental impacts of a road analyzed in the U.S. Fish and Wildlife Service's (Service) *King Cove Road—Briefing Report* dated August 1977 (Report). I request that a copy of the Report be included in the record of this hearing.

In summary, "The Service finds the road alternative contrary to the purposes of the refuge and foresees unacceptable environmental impacts if a road is constructed on refuge lands through the wilderness area. The Service supports further study and consideration of other alternatives, such as a marine link, which could provide increased safety, economic growth, and fewer ecological impacts."

The Report describes the likely effects of building and maintaining a road across or adjacent to wilderness habitats relied on by Pacific brant, emperor geese, Steller's eider (recently listed as a threatened species under the Endangered Species Act), tundra swan, brown bear, caribou, anadromous fish, wolf, wolverine, harbor seal, and sea otter. These species share a common need for minimal disturbance by humans, and for intact, pristine habitats now amply provided by the Izembek Wilderness.

A road that would bring increased human presence and disturbance for consumptive and non-consumptive purposes is incompatible with the habitat requirements of these species. For example, the Report notes that "The proposed road would have a significant impact on the habitat use, seasonal distribution, and survival of the southern Alaska Peninsula caribou herd," a herd now recovering from an alarmingly low level.

A road through the refuge wilderness could also lead to illegal off-road vehicle use, and the Service would find it difficult to protect sensitive refuge habitats and wildlife from such off-road use. In general, the Alaska experience has been that new roads pushed into previously roadless country soon lead to new illegal off-road vehicle trails and tracks, with consequent damage to terrain, increased poaching, and general disturbance to wildlife. Land management agencies typically lack the personnel to adequately monitor and enforce regulations against this illegal and destructive use.

The Sierra Club agrees with the Service's analysis in its Report and its recommendation for further study and consideration of alternatives.

S. 1092 versus the State's Transportation Planning Effort

A study of the purpose and need to improve King Cove-Cold Bay transportation is currently being done by the Alaska Department of Transportation and Public Facilities (DOT&PF) as part of its Alaska peninsula Intermodal Transportation Project.

As part of its overall King Cove-Cold Bay study, the Department intends to publish this fall an economic analysis of 6 alternative ways of improving transportation between the two communities. These alternatives are: 1. No-action, i.e., continue to rely on existing air service and private boats; 2. A new ferry linking the communities; 3. A road between the two communities that would cross Izembek Refuge; 4. A road from King Cove to a new airport north of Mt. Dutton; 5. Hovercraft service; and 6. An emergency "medivac" helicopter [presumably based in Cold Bay] to serve King Cove, False Pass, Port Moller, and perhaps other communities and residents. As a strict benefit-cost analysis, the study does not take into account environmental impacts.

This economic analysis will be considered along with other pertinent information and additional public comment to determine if there is a need for improved transportation between King Cove and Cold Bay, and if so, to identify the purposes of such improvement. In the end, the analysis could lead to the selection of a preferred alternative and the preparation of an environmental impact statement.

In October 1994, DOT&PF, as part of its Alaska Peninsula Intermodal Transportation Project, published a *Reconnaissance Study Report—King Cove-Cold Bay Access* that found a ferry alternative approximately equal in feasibility to a trans-refuge road. Ferry service was also found safer than the road alternative, and to be the most reliable means of travel between the two communities. Overall, based on 7 criteria, the ferry alternative scored 19 points, the road alternative 20.

The Sierra Club and other involved environmental organizations would like to see the State's transportation planning process proceed unhindered by attempts to provide undue advantage to one alternative or another—in this case S. 1092's attempt to facilitate the selection of a trans-refuge road.

Based on preliminary studies by DOT&PF, and the U.S. Fish and Wildlife Service's environmental analysis, the ferry alternative appears to offer an economically feasible, safe, reliable, and environmentally benign transportation link for the two communities, one that would achieve the desired economic, community development, and health and safety objectives. And it would avoid conflict with vital State, national, and international conservation objectives of Izembek National Wildlife Refuge and Izembek State Wildlife Refuge.

In short, the ferry alternative appears to offer superior advantages for all involved. We are confident that this conclusion will emerge from the State's planning process. As we have earlier indicated to King Cove and Borough representatives, we would actively support an effort to bring new ferry service to the two communities.

Meanwhile, we recommend that the Committee take no further action on S. 1092 in the interest of facilitating the orderly completion of the State's transportation planning process.

Thank you for this opportunity to present our views.

The CHAIRMAN. Mr. Rogers, would you care to join us this morning at the end of the table and get your statement. We welcome you to the committee and look forward to your testimony.

STATEMENT OF JOHN ROGERS, DEPUTY DIRECTOR, U.S. FISH AND WILDLIFE SERVICE, DEPARTMENT OF THE INTERIOR

Mr. ROGERS. Thank you, Mr. Chairman. I appreciate the opportunity today to provide testimony on S. 1092. We understand and support your desire for safe transportation between Cold Bay and King Cove communities. But we strongly oppose S. 1092. If enacted, the Secretary of the Interior would recommend to the President that he veto S. 1092 because of the negative impact it would have on a fragile wilderness area within the Izembek National Wildlife Refuge, the bill's broad waivers from application of important environmental laws, and because there are other transportation alternatives currently under consideration by the State of Alaska.

S. 1092 would result in a perpetual right of way through the lands and waters of Izembek National Wildlife Refuge. The proposed corridor would travel through a narrow isthmus between Izembek and Kinzarof Lagoons while traversing 10 miles of refuge lands, including 7 miles of designated wilderness.

We are sympathetic to safe and economical transportation needs for remote communities in the State of Alaska, but at the same time we must also safeguard the resources of the National Wildlife

Refuge System. The Izembek Lagoon complex is vital habitat to hundreds of thousands of waterfowl, including the world's population of Emperor geese and the Pacific black brant. These waterfowl species depend on Izembek and Kinzarof Lagoons during spring and fall migrations. The undisturbed nature provides vital habitat for these species.

Over half of the world's population of threatened Steller's eiders also come to the Izembek Lagoon to molt and spend the winter in the security of tidal waters. Its extensive eel grass beds, among the largest in the world, provide the food necessary for this species to replenish the nutrients depleted by migration, molting, and brood rearing.

Construction and use of the proposed road as outlined in S. 1092 would disturb these unique waterfowl populations. Construction through this fragile environment would also result in increased silt loads and alter drainage patterns into Kinzarof Lagoon. Increased siltation will affect the health of the eel grass beds upon which these waterfowl species depend.

The proposed road would parallel the Joshua Green River system, a key brown bear denning area, and interrupt an important wintering and primary migration corridor of the southern Alaska peninsula caribou herd. Vehicular traffic and increased human presence will alter seasonal distributions and migration routes for this important species.

Construction of a road through this pristine wilderness area would not be compatible with the purposes for which the Izembek National Wildlife Refuge was established. We believe, however, that viable alternatives to a proposed road exist and warrant further evaluation. The Alaska Department of Transportation and Public Facilities is currently evaluating transportation alternatives. Some of these alternatives have the potential to provide safe, highly reliable, and environmentally compatible travel between the King Cove and Cold Bay communities. We urge the committee to allow the current process to continue so that all these alternatives may be considered.

The Service does not see the goals of safety for Alaskan citizens and conserving vital fish and wildlife populations and habitat of the Izembek National Wildlife Refuge as mutually exclusive. We support working within the framework of the existing public processes to reach a solution that provides safe and reliable transportation for the citizens of Alaska without compromising the ecological integrity of this pristine wildland area.

Mr. Chairman, that concludes my testimony. I would be happy to answer questions.

[The prepared statement of Mr. Rogers follows:]

PREPARED STATEMENT OF JOHN ROGERS, DEPUTY DIRECTOR, U.S. FISH AND WILDLIFE SERVICE, DEPARTMENT OF THE INTERIOR

Mr. Chairman, I appreciate the opportunity to provide testimony on S. 1092. Although we understand and support your desire to ensure safe transportation between the King Cove and Cold Bay communities, we strongly oppose S. 1092. If enacted, the Secretary of the Interior will recommend to the President that he veto S. 1092 because of the negative impact it would have on a fragile wilderness area within the Izembek National Wildlife Refuge, the bill's broad waivers from application of important environmental laws, and because there are other transportation alternatives currently under consideration by the State of Alaska.

S. 1092 would result in a perpetual right-of-way through the lands and waters of Izembek National Wildlife Refuge and Izembek Wilderness. This right-of-way would be for the purpose of constructing a public road, and constructing, operating, and maintaining utility-related fixtures between two rural communities located near the tip of the southern Alaska Peninsula. The proposed corridor would bisect a narrow isthmus between Izembek and Kinzarof Lagoons while traversing 10 miles of Refuge lands, including 7 miles of designated wilderness.

We are sympathetic to safe and economical transportation for remote communities in the State of Alaska. At the same time, we, as an agency, must also safeguard the resources of the National Wildlife Refuge System. The Izembek Lagoon complex is vital habitat to hundreds of thousands of waterfowl, including the world's population of the regal emperor goose and the Pacific black brant. These waterfowl species descend on Izembek and Kinzarof Lagoons during spring and fall migrations.

Each fall, approximately 150,000 Pacific black brant converge on these lagoons coming from distant breeding grounds in Russia, Canada and Alaska. In recent years, an increasing proportion of brant remain to over-winter on Kinzarof and Izembek Refuge Lagoons. The wilderness character of the Izembek Lagoon complex provides vital habitat for these species of international significance.

Over half of the world's population of the threatened Stellar's eider also flock to the Izembek Lagoons to molt and spend the winter in the security of the tidal waters. The extensive eelgrass beds, among the largest in the world, provide the food necessary for this species to replenish the nutrients depleted by migration, molting and brood rearing.

Construction and the use of the proposed road as outlined in S. 1092 would disturb these internationally-unique waterfowl populations. Construction through this fragile tundra environment would also result in increased silt loads and alter drainage patterns into Kinzarof Lagoon. Increased siltation will affect the health of the eelgrass beds upon which these waterfowl species depend.

The proposed road would also parallel the Joshua Green River system, a key brown bear denning area, and bisect an important wintering and primary migration corridor of the southern Alaska Peninsula Caribou Herd. Vehicular traffic and increased human presence will affect adversely seasonal distributions and migration routes for this important species.

Construction of a road through this pristine wilderness area would not be compatible with the purposes for which the Izembek National Wildlife Refuge was established. We believe, however, that viable alternatives to a proposed road exist and warrant further evaluation.

The Alaska Department of Transportation and Public Facilities (ADOT/PF) is currently evaluating transportation alternatives. Some of these alternatives have the potential to provide safe, highly reliable, and environmentally-compatible travel between the Cold Bay and King Cove communities. We urge further consideration of these alternatives.

The communities of King Cove and Cold Bay are separated by approximately 20 miles of marine waters that have provided passage between the communities for over 50 years. Enhancing the marine transportation and shipping facilities would provide improved safe travel to the entire region. Regularly scheduled ferry service between King Cove and Cold Bay would provide safe and reliable travel with fewer environmental impacts than a road.

The development of routine marine service would entail improving the docking facility at Cold Bay and providing a vessel equipped with state of the art navigational aids to travel between the two communities. In addition, improvements to air travel would also benefit the King Cove and Cold Bay communities. Relocating or upgrading the current air facility could greatly improve air access.

We are working cooperatively with the state in the consideration and planning of alternatives to meet the transportation needs of King Cove and the surrounding communities.

The Service does not see the goals of safety for Alaskan citizens and conserving vital fish and wildlife populations and habitat of the Izembek National Wildlife Refuge as mutually exclusive. We support working within the framework of existing public processes to reach a solution that provides safe and reliable transportation for the citizens of Alaska, without compromising the ecological integrity of this pristine wildland area.

In addition to the above concerns, the Administration strongly objects to language in Sections 4(c) and (e) that exempts the land exchange from requirements of the National Environmental Policy Act, 49 U.S.C. 303(c), the Alaska Native Claims Settlement Act, the Alaska National Interest Lands Conservation Act and the National Historic Preservation Act. Such exemptions undercut the applicability of the laws, undermine enforcement, possibly lead to serious environmental problems, and set a dangerous precedent by encouraging similar waivers.

Thank you for the opportunity to testify on S. 1092. I would be happy to answer any questions you may have.

The CHAIRMAN. Mr. Rogers, have you been out there?

Mr. ROGERS. I have not been to Cold Bay.

The CHAIRMAN. That is too bad. I always like to have a witness that knows what he is talking about.

If the State chooses a road access, would the U.S. Fish and Wildlife support it?

Mr. ROGERS. Sir, it is very difficult to respond to——

The CHAIRMAN. Just a yes or no.

Mr. ROGERS [continuing]. Hypotheticals, but——

The CHAIRMAN. Hypothetically, if the State chooses it, what is the U.S. Fish and Wildlife going to do?

Mr. ROGERS. The current situation presents us with an absolute. That is, there is going to be a road, and we unalterably oppose this current legislation. If, however, a road emerges as the preferred alternative, I would assume that there would be a specific proposal associated with it.

The CHAIRMAN. Yes, it is 6 or 7 miles of road extension through the wilderness.

Mr. ROGERS. And we would look at the——

The CHAIRMAN. And the question is quite simple. Are you going to support it or not? Your facts are going to be the same, if they are facts at all.

Mr. ROGERS. Our process, once we knew the details of the road in terms of construction standards, specific locations, and maintenance, would allow us to come to a more specific compatibility determination.

The CHAIRMAN. Well, that is a bureaucratic answer and you and I both know it.

Mr. ROGERS. It would be a very high hurdle to climb.

The CHAIRMAN. What are you going to do about the road, the 5 or 6 miles of wilderness road that you have got there now that are there?

Mr. ROGERS. Those were in existence prior to designation as a wilderness.

The CHAIRMAN. Yes, but they are used. They are used.

Mr. ROGERS. I understand that.

The CHAIRMAN. Does that have any effect on your concern?

Mr. ROGERS. They are not routinely used and maintained as a transportation corridor. They are internal roads that are used only occasionally.

The CHAIRMAN. Well, you know what? Let us assume that you were a young U.S. Fish and Wildlife Service employee in King Cove and you were married, and your wife was stricken at night in the fall and the only access was to try and get her out in a small airplane. We have heard one of the witnesses who had that experience. And you were 6 miles away from a road. What would your attitude be?

Mr. ROGERS. I understand the difficulties of travel on the Alaska peninsula in emergency situations, and that is why the Fish and Wildlife Service fully supports the State process that is under way to develop and identify the most effective and efficient and reliable means of emergency transportation.

The CHAIRMAN. Well, you know, the State's process, while ongoing, is rather curious, too, because—I am quoting a Friday, June 16, statement by the Knowles administration made in a speech to the Rotary Club in Juneau. This is a statement by the Governor as an example of how roads could boost local economics. Now, this is not the health and safety. "The Governor noted a planned 20-mile road between King Cove and Cold Bay that would allow salmon caught near King Cove to be delivered quickly to Cold Bay's 10,000 foot jet runway, putting the fresh fish onto the international market more quickly. The Governor suggested changing Alaska's transportation policy to include more coordination with local governments and the public in building local roads that feed into the Federal highways in Alaska."

So I would suggest to you that, while the State is proceeding with a study, which I commend them for, there has been some indication by the State administration relative to this subject.

Are you familiar with R.S. 2477?

Mr. ROGERS. Roughly, yes.

The CHAIRMAN. Well, it is pretty important to Alaskans because that is the law that ensures that we have access across public land if indeed it had been used as a thoroughfare or for some kind of a regular transportation route, including a footpath.

I believe there is a chart over here that shows the access routes, and I wonder, Mr. Hoff, if you could indicate—I think you are pretty much a pioneer, Marvin, of the area?

Mr. HOFF. Yes, sir.

The CHAIRMAN. Does this route, footpath of trappers, pretty much follow the shoreline and the proposed road extension 6 to 7 miles that you would propose to access?

Mr. HOFF. As you can see, in the 1800's, 1900's, there was numerous trapping cabins throughout the Cold Bay area. All these trappers hiked to and from King Cove, in the 1900's, that is, after most all the Aleuts moved to King Cove for the cannery and the schools.

The CHAIRMAN. So it is fair to say that there has been trapping and so forth on that routing for some time?

Mr. HOFF. Sir, they hiked along the shoreline and hiked, and they trapped and hunted.

The CHAIRMAN. What I find rather curious, and I think it is going to be an ideal opportunity for the administration to stand up and be counted, is they have always told us they do not need R.S. 2477, but if we have a legitimate need for a road across public lands, why, simply make the appeal based on the merits. So I would encourage the administration to look at the merits relative to either R.S. 2477 or the reality that these people are within 6 or 7 miles of road access through a wilderness and a total of, what do they need, 17 or 18 miles to hook up the village of King Cove.

Are there any U.S. Fish and Wildlife Service in King Cove?

Mr. ROGERS. I do not believe we have any permanent personnel.

The CHAIRMAN. Do you know why?

Mr. ROGERS. No, I do not.

The CHAIRMAN. That might be a reason, the safety of your personnel. Yet there is 600 to 700 Alaska constituents out there that have a terrible time when they have to get out. You know, if one of you, as I have been out there many, many times—it is a beautiful, unique area, but to suggest that 6 or 7 miles of additional road are somehow going to befoul the area contradicts reality.

The eel grass is there. The fragile environment is there. It is going to be limited to a very small group of very hardy Alaskans who make their living in this very harsh area. To suggest that when you go in there—it is wild and woolly country, so as far as a concern over an extended population, I think that is unrealistic.

Mr. Hession, did we not have an accident with some of the Sierra Club folks not so long ago up in ANWR?

Mr. HESSION. I am not aware of that, Mr. Chairman.

The CHAIRMAN. I thought we had to bring a helicopter in to fly some of the Sierra Club people out in an emergency.

Mr. HESSION. I am not aware of that, but I would be happy to look into it.

The CHAIRMAN. Okay. Well, I will try before the hearing is over to provide you with the information.

Do we have it here? This is "Visiting hiker drowned in North Slope river. The accident occurred in the Sadlerochit River 280 miles southeast of Barrow. According to borough police, Forsythe"—excuse me. "According to Borough Police Corporal Jim Beckham, Forsythe was with a party of 12 hikers on a Sierra Club-sponsored trip." I am surprised you do not know about it, Jack. "The group was attempting to cross the river at a spot scattered with sandbars. Beckham said the group apparently misread a section of the river that ran deep and fast. 'Forsythe was overcome by the current,' he said. 'The rest of the group said that they eventually had to form a human chain to get themselves across,' Beckham said. The hikers recovered the victim's body about 21½ miles downstream. The group used a flare gun to catch the attention of a private helicopter pilot in the area. The pilot radioed authorities."

I wonder if you feel any differently about helicopters in wilderness areas?

Mr. HESSION. We have always supported the use of helicopters for emergency rescues in wilderness areas. It is provided for under existing Federal law. There is no problem there at all.

The CHAIRMAN. Oh, yes, there is a big problem with Federal agencies, and there is a lot. We have had situations in many areas of the State where they have been challenged about going into these areas because of the concern over bringing a helicopter into a wilderness. So to suggest that just because it is in the law it is not challenged——

Mr. HESSION. Mr. Chairman, I would urge you to have your staff look into that. I know of no case in which a Federal——

The CHAIRMAN. I will give you the cases. There is a case in southeastern Alaska in the Tongass where the Forest Service challenged Tempsco for trying to rescue a hunter 6 or 7 years ago. That one just comes to mind. There have been a couple in Denali. So we will provide you with the information.

But I think we have got a consistency here relative to the safety and access, and to suggest that there is not justification for this road, particularly when the State administration seems to have moved a little bit from the statement that was originally given, at least at the Rotary Club meeting, to a situation of studying the area—and I think, Jack, you were out there the other day, were you not?

Mr. HESSION. Yes, sir, I have made two visits.

The CHAIRMAN. You went by boat this time.

Mr. HESSION. By boat. We got out on foot. We looked at the airport at King Cove, generally took a brief but comprehensive tour.

The CHAIRMAN. You think you could have gotten off your boat if you had not had the unique opportunity to have a 250-foot freighter provide you a breaker so you could get off?

Mr. HESSION. In Cold Bay?

The CHAIRMAN. Yes.

Mr. HESSION. It would have probably been more difficult, I will say that, Mr. Chairman.

The CHAIRMAN. And you could not fly that day, could you?

Mr. HESSION. From King Cove, the judgment was that it was inadvisable to fly.

The CHAIRMAN. You can appreciate this is pretty tough country?

Mr. HESSION. I will acknowledge that Cold Bay could use a breakwater or a small boat harbor, an obvious need there.

The CHAIRMAN. Yes, but what are you going to do when you cross, when you get outside the breakwater? You have got the reality of a pretty tough——

Mr. HESSION. At times, certainly, Senator. But as you know from your experience in southeast Alaska and from other experience in this country, high speed ferries can handle very severe weather conditions and sea conditions.

The CHAIRMAN. Sure they can.

Mr. HESSION. I have been on them myself.

The CHAIRMAN. Well, I hope the Federal Government and the Sierra Club will help us finance a ferry, because I do not think the State will.

I have got to go vote, so I am going to ask Gregg Renkes to proceed with this process, and I will do the best I can.

Mr. MALNAK. Why do we not, Mr. Rogers, while we have you up, follow up on some of the questions that the chairman has for you. First of all, was this road not proposed as part of the Bristol Bay cooperative management plan which was directed to be prepared by the committee as part of the Alaska Lands Act?

Mr. ROGERS. I understand it was.

Mr. MALNAK. Was the Service opposed to the road as part of that act?

Mr. ROGERS. My understanding is yes.

Mr. MALNAK. What is the history of enforcement of the wilderness boundary at Izembek Lagoon?

Mr. ROGERS. I cannot speak directly to that. There is considerable access by both recreational users and subsistence users to both the wilderness and the rest of the refuge.

Mr. MALNAK. Is it true that the Service has not until recently rigorously enforced the wilderness boundary as to vehicular traffic, and that for many years vehicles did enter the refuge for recreation uses on roads which were previously built in the wilderness?

Mr. ROGERS. I cannot speak to that, I am sorry.

Mr. MALNAK. Would you see if you can get that for the record?

Mr. ROGERS. Yes.

Mr. MALNAK. Thank you.

The next question would be for Della Trumble. Could you tell us what the situation is with how you handle pregnant women on the island and what they have to go through?

Ms. TRUMBLE. The majority of the pregnant women, we do have health aides in King Cove. We do have some nurse practitioners. In any event that there is any complications or any possibility of complications, these women are removed from the community by up to 2 months in time. In a normal situation, it is a minimum of 3 weeks. They do not have the capability of doing any other medical services in King Cove except to stabilize any situation.

Just to give you an example of this, I have had a niece that was born—my sister-in-law had gone into labor at 7 months and had to get out of King Cove in a probably 50, 60 mile an hour wind. She was born halfway to Cold Bay on the galley table, and they used an electric heater and foil wrap to make a makeshift incubator.

Getting her off the dock on a stretcher in Cold Bay, with the wind blowing, her IV got caught under that dock. That dock is 20 to 30 feet high.

Mr. Hession made a point that it was easy for him to get off. He has been to the cove a couple times. And I am glad he enjoyed and got to have the adventure of doing it two times. We put up with this every day. It is continuous. Any of form of transportation is not going to work. We are still fighting all the elements.

Mr. MALNAK. Thank you.

Mr. Hennigh, one final question. We have heard about some of the other alternatives that are being discussed. What is the viability of those alternatives and what is your feeling about any other alternative to air transportation?

Mr. HENNIGH. Well, my opinion is that the only alternative that makes any common sense in a both quantitative and qualitative evaluation sense is a road. The thing that we cannot mitigate in this whole mess is the weather, and it is the weather that will impact anything that you might want to do—with the current aviation mode, with a helicopter, with boats. Mother Nature simply has the final say there.

Money spent on anything but a road would be money poorly spent by whoever's money it is. A road is not a 100 percent answer, but it is the closest thing that we have got to a 100 percent answer, and without a doubt it is the only alternative that intuitively makes sense to those of us who live out there.

Mr. RENKES. Thank you. I am going to dismiss the panel now and move on to S. 660. Thank you very much for your time, patience, testimony, and sorry for the jump in the process this morning, but it is out of our control.

I would like to ask up Dr. Komisar, Bart Koehler, and Kevin Tritt first. We will try to get the folks that have traveled here from a long way away. Then I hope it is okay for the Department or the Bureau of Land Management, Mr. Fry, to wait until the end, and we will definitely get your testimony.

[Pause.]

Mr. RENKES. I think Dr. Komisar stepped out for a minute. In the interest of meeting our time constraints, Bart, why do you not start, and try to keep it to about 5 minutes and then we will move through it. If there is more time later, then we will pick up and try to give you more time.

STATEMENT OF BART KOEHLER, EXECUTIVE DIRECTOR, SOUTHEAST ALASKA CONSERVATION COUNCIL, JUNEAU, AK

Mr. KOEHLER. Thank you, Mr. Chairman. I have not seen you in that chair seat before, so it is an interesting phenomenon, I am sure.

My name is Bart Koehler and I am the executive director of the Southeast Alaska Conservation Council, and I will summarize my statement and hopefully the whole thing will be put in the record. I will be throwing some numbers and dates around, so please try to bear with me on this.

SEACC strongly opposes S. 660 because it directly attacks the Tongass National Forest, it attacks our national forest and public lands heritage, and because the State of Alaska has already gotten enough land from the Federal Government. This public land give-away would allow a university to select at least 250,000 acres of national forest and other Federal lands in Alaska that are not "conservation system units."

This bill threatens the legislated LUD II areas set aside by the Tongass Timber Reform Act, areas that Senators Murkowski and Stevens and 97 other U.S. Senators voted to protect in perpetuity in 1990.

Based on its history, the university will select lands that they can turn into cash fast. They will target Tongass old growth timber lands and hammer them.

Mr. Chairman, Alaskan support for protecting legislated LUD II areas runs wide and deep. That was true during the Reform Act days and it is true now. So far, ten southeast Alaskan communities and two tribal governments have gone on record opposing this legislation. Other groups, like the Alaska Outdoor Council and others, have also gone on record in opposition. These Alaskans do not want their national forest lands given to the University of Alaska.

Senator Murkowski tried to pass a similar bill last year. At least last year's bill did not allow the selection of any national forests in Alaska, thus eliminating the problem of selecting legislated LUD II areas and other lands in the Tongass and Chugach National Forests.

We also need to set the record straight today. The University owns more than 111,000 acres. It currently holds title to 140,000 acres of fee simple land. It also holds in total 173,000 acres of investment property.

Senator Murkowski claims that Alaska ranks 48th among the States for Federal land given to its university. Alaska also ranks 49th among the States for population, and it should be noted that the Morrill Act, those grants were based on population.

We should note that for every current Alaska resident the Federal Government has given one-fifth of an acre to the university. This is 31 times the amount of land given to the University of California for every resident of that State. For every student at the University of Alaska, the Federal Government has given Alaska almost five acres. This is roughly four times the amount of land given to the University of California students.

In 1862 the Morrill Act grants were based on population, not on the total State acreage. If Alaska had been granted university lands under the Morrill Act, it would have received 90,000 acres.

As a result of the Act of 1915, which is cited in the findings of this legislation, roughly 11,000 acres were transferred to the university before the Federal land grant was revoked by the Statehood Act. In 1929 Congress granted 100,000 acres to the university. In 1958, with the passage of statehood, the university's grants were consolidated into the Statehood Act and the Statehood Act extinguished all land entitlements for Alaska.

We must point out that Alaska was granted 104 million acres of Federal land under the Statehood Act. That is 104 million acres. That is an area bigger than the State of California. Nineteen States received less than one million acres each. Twenty-one States received 10 million acres down to 2.7 million acres. If Senator Campbell was still here, Colorado received 4 million acres.

Alaska in our minds should be the last State in the Union to ever receive more Federal public land. Yet Alaska got even more land later. In 1980, section 906(b) of ANILCA granted the State of Alaska an additional 75,000 acres as "full and final settlement of any and all claims by the State of Alaska arising under the Act of March 4, 1915." We have never seen this act mentioned in Senator Murkowski's opening statement. We believe that this provision pertains to university land claims under the 1915 Act, and by our calculations Congress granted Alaska 186,000 acres of Federal land. That would rank Alaska as number 34 instead of number 48.

And I repeat, the 1980 provision was supposed to be the full and final settlement of any and all claims by the State of Alaska arising under the 1915 Act.

Mr. Chairman—since you are not Senator Murkowski I cannot call you Senator—Alaska, as you know, has no State income tax. It gives away $1,000 or more each year to every man, woman and child as a Permanent Fund dividend. It was granted 104 million acres, far more than any other State. Two governors of Alaska have vetoed bills to grant State lands to the university. If governors of Alaska do not want to grant State land to the university, then why on earth should the Congress be asked to grant large tracts of public land instead?

If the University of Alaska needs more funding, and their budget has been slashed year after year recently by the State legislature, then they should get it from the State legislature. By no means should the University of Alaska be allowed to raid the public's lands and the public's national forests, not the Tongass, not the Chugach, not anywhere.

Finally, if this bill passes it will set the dangerous precedent of raiding and dismantling our national forest system, a living legacy of great importance to the American people. Teddy Roosevelt once said: "I oppose the land-skinner every time." If Teddy were here to see how the University of Alaska has skinned off the land they have managed and heard that this bill was trying to give the university hundreds of thousands of acres from our national forests in Alaska, national forests that Teddy established in 1907, I am convinced that this bill would be stopped dead in its tracks.

That is the end of my statement. It is our view that this is not a land grant, this is a public land grab, and we oppose it, as do many national conservation groups, including the Wilderness Society, Sierra Club, Alaska Wilderness League, and the Republicans for Environmental Protection.

Thank you.

[The prepared statement of Mr. Koehler follows:]

PREPARED STATEMENT OF BART KOEHLER, EXECUTIVE DIRECTOR, SOUTHEAST ALASKA CONSERVATION COUNCIL, JUNEAU, AK

Mr. Chairman, and members of this committee, my name is Bart Koehler, and I am the Executive Director for the Southeast Alaska Conservation Council (SEACC). I respectfully request that my written statement and accompanying materials be entered into the official record of this committee hearing.

Founded in 1970, SEACC is a coalition of 15 local citizen, volunteer conservation groups in 12 Southeast Alaska communities, from Ketchikan to Yakutat. SEACC's individual members include commercial fishermen, Alaskan Natives, small timber operators and value-added wood manufacturers, tourism and recreation business owners, hunters, guides, and Alaskans from all walks of life. SEACC is dedicated to preserving the integrity of Southeast Alaska's unsurpassed natural environment while providing for balanced, sustainable use of our region's resources.

THE ALASKA DELEGATION'S FRONTAL ASSAULT ON THE TONGASS NATIONAL FOREST

After proposing 17 unsuccessful legislative initiatives to roll back Tongass reforms in the last Congress, the Alaska Delegation is once again trying to open up the Tongass to increased logging. See Exhibit 1.* Senate Bill 660 is yet another attack in an unprecedented assault aimed at rolling back balanced management provisions, and undermining the Tongass Timber Reform Act (TTRA) which passed the Senate by a resounding 99-0 vote. Once again, the Alaska Delegation is attempting to take large chunks of the Tongass and dedicate these public forest lands to some massive exploitation scheme. With each new bill, the tactics change but the goal remains the same—attack the Tongass.

SEACC opposes S. 660

SEACC strongly opposes S. 660, because it is directly attacking the Tongass, because it is an assault on our National Forests and public lands, and because the State of Alaska has already gotten enough land from the Federal Government.

On April 28, 1997, Senator Murkowski introduced S. 660, the "University of Alaska Lands (Grab) Bill." This public land giveaway would allow the University to select at least 250,000 acres of National Forests and other federal lands within Alaska that are not "conservation system units" (conservation system units as defined in ANILCA (Public Law 96-487) include National Parks, National Wildlife Refuges, National Monuments, and Wilderness Areas). This bill threatens the Legislated LUD II areas set aside by the Tongass Timber Reform Act—areas that Senators Murkowski and Stevens and 97 other U.S. Senators voted to protect "in perpetuity" in 1990. And that's not all: up to 250,000 additional acres of National Forest and other Federal lands could be selected if matched by an equal acreage from State lands. Under this bill, half a million acres of public land, including lands within the Tongass National Forest, could be selected for clearcutting and other damaging uses.

This bill threatens 723,000 acres of wildlands important to Southeast communities and citizens for commercial and sport fishing, subsistence and sport hunting, recreation, and other uses. These important fish and wildlife watersheds were "permanently" set off limits to logging in the 1990 TTRA. Now, Senator Murkowski is willing to sacrifice these critical areas for one purpose—creating income for the University of Alaska.

Forced to squeeze as much revenue out of their lands as possible, the University has never acted as careful stewards. The University will select lands which they can turn into cash fast—they will target Tongass old-growth timber lands and level

---

*The exhibits and attachments have been retained in committee files.

them as quickly as possible. The University does not manage for multiple use, instead they manage their lands much like private lands—laying down massive clearcuts and exporting round logs, while placing the absolute minimum protections on fish and wildlife habitat.

This bill threatens the following Tongass areas:

- Wildlands protected by the Tongass Timber Reform Act that weren't designated as "conservation system units" (this includes all the Legislated LUD II areas). The University could select from these 723,000 acres of prime old-growth forests important for fish and wildlife habitat—places like Kadashan, Naha, Nutkwa, Berners Bay, Point Adolphus/Mud Bay, Lisianski Inlet, Calder-Holbrook, Salmon Bay Lake, Anan Creek, Trap Bay, Outside Islands, Upper Hoonah Sound, and the Yakutat Forelands.
- Unprotected Tongass wildlands important to Southeast Alaska communities, including: Cleveland Peninsula, Port Houghton, Mansfield Peninsula, Honker Divide, East Kuiu, Ushk Bay, Deep Bay, and Upper Tenakee Inlet.

Alaskan support for protecting TTRA Legislated LUD II areas runs wide and deep. Fifteen Southeast Alaskan communities, the State of Alaska, 5 Native organizations, the statewide United Fishermen of Alaska and all of Southeast Alaska's regional commercial fishing organizations, plus many other groups and individuals, have been on record in support of protecting these important fish and wildlife watersheds. Furthermore, Alaska Senators Murkowski and Stevens and 97 other U.S. Senators voted to protect these very same areas.

This bill, as currently written, contains no provision which would exclude these TTRA Legislated LUD II areas and lands set aside by the new Tongass National Forest Plan Revision, or other Tongass National Forest lands from selection by the University.

So far, 10 S.E. Alaskan Communities and 2 Tribal Governments have gone on record opposing this legislation.

Senator Murkowski tried to gain passage of a similar bill last year, during the Omnibus Parks Bill debate. At the very least, last year's final and unsuccessful version of this bill did not allow the selection of any National Forest lands in Alaska. Last year's language eliminated the problem of selecting the TTRA Legislated LUD II areas and other key lands in the Tongass National Forest and Chugach National Forest.

Setting the record straight

University Owns More Than 112,000 Acres: Much has been made of the point that Alaska only received 112,000 acres for its land grant university, and that Alaska ranks 48th among the States for federal land given to its system of higher education. First of all, the University of Alaska holds title to roughly 140,000 acres of fee simple land. That acreage figure would give Alaska a higher ranking than Senator Murkowski has indicated. Second, when you add in all of the University's land trust holdings, including fee simple lands (140,223 acres), surface rights only (16,585 acres), subsurface rights only (1,020 acres), harvestable timber only (15,000 acres), and agricultural rights only (789 acres), you see that the University currently holds 173,326 acres of investment property—much more than the 112,000 acres cited by Senator Murkowski.

Alaska Was Actually Granted 186,000 Acres By Congress: Based on grants made by Congress in 1915, 1929, and 1980, the State of Alaska was granted 186,000 acres of land for higher education. (see discussion of Federal Grants, below). Senator Murkowski never has mentioned the grant of 75,000 acres in Sec. 906(b) of ANILCA in 1980. The 186,000 acres of federal lands grant total would then rank Alaska as #34, just below California and Arkansas, and above 17 other states.

The Morrill Act Federal Land Grants Were Based on Population: While Senator Murkowski claims that Alaska ranks 48th among the states for federal land given to its university system (according to the figures provided by Sen. Murkowski in the April 28, 1997 Congressional Record), Alaska also ranks 49th among the states for population (1990 U.S. Census). The Morrill Act grants were based on population. For every current Alaska resident the federal government has given 1/5 of an acre of land to the University of Alaska system. This is almost twice the per capita amount given to Rhode Island residents for their higher education system, 3 times the amount given to Washington state residents, almost 4 times the amount given to New York state residents, 19 times the amount given to Texas residents, and 31 times the amount of land given to the University of California for every resident of that state.

Look At the Number of Students: Only 23,354 students are enrolled in the University of Alaska system statewide. That means for every student, the federal government has given Alaska almost 5 acres of federal land—this is roughly 4 times the amount of land given to University of California students, each of which is supported by 1.2 acres of federal land grant (with at least 165,000 students in the U.C. System.)

Federal Land Grants

1862 and the Morrill Act: The Alaska Delegation has noted that in 1862, the Morrill Act passed, "which created the land-grant colleges and universities as a way to underwrite the cost of higher education . . . . these colleges and universities received land from the Federal Government for facility location and. . . . as a way to provide for sustaining revenues to those educational institutions." Then they went on to note that "The grants were based on population as measured by the size of the delegation with each state receiving approximately 30,000 acres per member." If Alaska had been granted university lands under the Morrill Act, it would have received 90,000 acres.

In 1915, while still a territory, Alaska Delegate James Wickersham pushed a measure through Congress which set aside approximately 250,000 acres in the Tanana Valley to support an agricultural college and school of mines. However, the land could not be transferred to the college until it was surveyed. Eventually, roughly 11,000 acres were transferred to the University of Alaska before the federal land grant was revoked.

In 1929, while still a territory, Congress granted 100,000 acres to the Alaska Agriculture College and School of Mines.

In 1958, Congress granted Alaska Statehood and according to Alaska Delegation statements, . . . "with the passage of Statehood the 'internal improvement grants' including the (hoped-for) University's 500,000 acres and 500,000 acres for the University's teacher training programs (these grants were part of the statehood bills during the 1950s) were consolidated into the 100-million-acre general grant, leaving disposition of all 102+ million acres at the discretion of the legislature. Passage of the Statehood bill virtually ended all discussion of federal land grants." The Statehood Act extinguished all land entitlements for Alaska, including the Morrill Act.

We must point out that Alaska was granted 104 million acres of federal land under the Statehood Act. (That's a land area bigger than the State of California) 19 States received less than 1 million acres each of federal land. (Alaska got at least 100 times more land than these States.) 21 States received from 10 million acres down to 2.7 million acres. (Alaska got 10 times to almost 50 times more land than these States.) Given these facts, we submit that Alaska should be the last State in the Union to ever receive more federal public land from Congress. Yet, Alaska got even more land later.

1980—Congress Grants Alaska Another 75,000 Acres for Education: As if the 104-million-acre Statehood Grant wasn't enough, Section 906(b) of ANILCA (Public Law 96-487) granted the State of Alaska an additional 75,000 acres as a "full and final settlement of any and all claims by the State of Alaska arising under the Act of March 4, 1915 (38 Stat. 1214), as confirmed and transferred in section 6(k) of the Alaska Statehood Act . . ." In our minds, this definitely refers to University of Alaska land claims. This School Lands Settlement provision granted 75,000 acres from vacant, unappropriated and unreserved public lands. The State was entitled to select these lands until January 4, 1994. The provision then went on to state, "In exercising the selection rights granted herein, the State shall be deemed to have relinquished all claims to any right, title or interest to any school lands which failed to vest under the above statutes at the time Alaska became a State (January 3, 1959), including lands unsurveyed at that date or surveyed lands which were within Federal reservations or withdrawals on that date."

Senator Murkowski's introductory statement never mentions this provision of ANILCA. We believe that this provision pertains to University land claims under the 1915 Act. By our calculations, acts of Congress in 1915, 1929, and 1980 granted the State of Alaska 186,000 acres of Federal Land for the University of Alaska's educational needs. And the 1980 provision was supposed to be the "full and final settlement of any and all claims by the State of Alaska arising under the Act of March 4, 1915 . . ." The 1915 Act granted lands for the University, and the 1929 Act granted more lands to the University. Later, the Statehood Act extinguished further land grants, and then in 1980, after granting even more lands, ANILCA extinguished further land grants again.

Telling comments

Senator Murkowski made two telling comments in his introductory statement . . . . "The University of Alaska received the smallest amount of land of any State, with the exception of Delaware" (and Hawaii didn't get a single acre) and then went on to say, "In a State the size of Alaska . . . . we should logically have one of the best and most fully funded land-grant colleges in the country." He completely misses three points: 1) that the University land grants were based on population size, not the total acreage of the state; 2) that the 1915 and 1929 Acts and the generous 104-million-acre Statehood grant to Alaska (which extinguished any land claims) should have provided the State of Alaska with ways to properly fund its own University system without needing any more federal land grants; and, 3) that Alaska was granted another 75,000 acres of federal land for schools as part of the "full and final settlement of any and all claims by the State of Alaska . . ." in ANILCA in 1980. Clearly, Alaska has gotten enough Federal Land.

Alaska Is Rich in Resources: It has no State income tax, it gives away roughly $1,000 each year for every man, woman and child in the State as a permanent fund dividend, and it was granted 104 million acres of land . . . far more than any other State. More than one Governor of Alaska has vetoed bills to grant State lands to the University. If Governors of Alaska don't want to grant State land to the University, then why on earth should the Congress be asked to grant large tracts of public lands instead?

We've heard a lot about the University of Alaska's financial woes. In recent years the Alaska State Legislature has slashed millions of dollars from the University's budget. If the University of Alaska needs more funding, then they should get it from the State legislature. By no means should the University of Alaska be allowed to raid the public's lands and the public's National Forests—not on the Tongass, not on the Chugach, not anywhere.

So now, almost 40 years after Statehood extinguished all land entitlements for Alaska, and almost 20 years since ANILCA extinguished them again, why the push for this legislation? We submit that with their powerful positions in Congress, the Alaska Delegation sees this as a golden opportunity to strike at the heart of lands protected by the Tongass Timber Reform Act and to try to pull off a land grab in our largest National Forest.

Dismantling our national forest heritage

This issue is far bigger than just a simple transfer of public lands in Alaska to the University of Alaska. If this bill passes, it will set the dangerous precedent of raiding and dismantling our National Forest System—a living legacy of great importance to the American people. This bill will take this public lands legacy out of the public's hands, and give those lands to a diversity which has a terrible track record of huge damaging clearcuts in Alaska. (Also, the University's track record shows it would be busy chopping up those former public lands into "waterfront and scenic view" lots to sell off to private owners).

Teddy Roosevelt once said, "I oppose the land-skinner every time." If Teddy were here to see how the University of Alaska has skinned off the land they've managed, and heard that Senator Murkowski was trying to give the University of Alaska hundreds of thousands of acres from our National Forests in Alaska—National Forests that Teddy established in 1907—I'm convinced that this bill would be stopped dead in its tracks.

We feel very strongly about even thinking about taking the public lands out of the public's hands . . . . particularly our National Forest lands. During the last Congress, Representative Don Young introduced a bill which proposed giving the Tongass National Forest to the State of Alaska. At that time we stated, "the bill is striking at the very heart of the century-old, all-American concept of public forest lands. To many Americans, the concept of being an owner of our public National Forest lands is one of our most strongly held freedoms. This is a freedom where Alaskans can pick a spot on the Tongass map, climb into a float plane or skiff and go there. They can hunt, fish, hike and camp. When they leave, they leave with the knowledge that they can return to the same spot on their public land, again and again. This is a freedom that we hold dear and you want to rip it away."

This statement rings true today, and therefore we must strongly oppose passage of S. 660.

Mr. RENKES. Thank you, Mr. Koehler.
Dr. Komisar.

STATEMENT OF DR. JEROME B. KOMISAR, PRESIDENT, UNIVERSITY OF ALASKA, FAIRBANKS, AK

Dr. KOMISAR. Mr. Chairman, thank you. I am Jerome E. Komisar, president of the University of Alaska, and I am very pleased to be here to present the university's views in support of

S. 660, which would grant Federal public lands to the university, fulfilling earlier commitments made to it by Congress.

The University of Alaska is Alaska's only public land grant university. In 1915 and 1929, Congress made Federal land grants totaling close to 370,000 acres to the Territory of Alaska for the exclusive use and benefit of the university. For a number of reasons, the university has received less than a third of the acreage allocated to it under these grants.

The failure to transfer the total allotment was due to the incompleteness of the Federal Government's study of the region. Before they could be conveyed, the lands had to be surveyed. As of 1915, only a fraction of 1 percent of Alaska had been surveyed, virtually none of it in the Tanana Valley where the granted lands were located.

As late as 1952, a mere six-tenths of a percent of the entire Territory of Alaska had been surveyed. In the early 1950's, predictions about how long it would take to survey Alaska at current Federal speed varied between 12,000 and 43,510 years.

The result of all of this is that, of all the States that have received land grants, only Delaware received less than Alaska and, given the size of Alaska, no other State by far received a smaller portion of total State acreage for the support of higher learning.

This obvious inequity is impossible to rationalize. First, Alaska's vast size makes it eminently possible to devote significant acreage to the support of higher education and greater learning. Alaska does not have a land shortage, at least not in public lands.

Second, Alaska's vast distances, its remote harsh climate, its harsh climatic conditions, and the remote locations of many of its cities and villages create prohibitive costs unknown in the rest of the country, which makes a grant of land exemplary public policy. If there is any section of our Nation where educational land grants are justified and necessary, it is in the great land of Alaska.

The University of Alaska is a statewide system which consists of three multi-mission universities located in Anchorage, Fairbanks, and Juneau, with extended satellite colleges and centers including over dozens of extension and research sites. Not surprisingly, the need for higher education is most difficult to serve in the rural and remote areas of the State, where vast distances separate cities and villages, where air travel is the only means of transportation, and where the cost of communications—telephone, television, electronic networks—can be exorbitant.

A sufficient land grant would enable the university to plan and provide more effectively the educational and cultural services needed throughout the enormous Alaska terrain and would permit the massive size of the land to provide economic benefits as well as cause financial costs.

Additional land will also enable the university to further the application of exemplary ways of extracting and managing natural resources.

It will permit economic development projects and land utilization that balance environmental protection with social progress. The income earned will further the university's research in those disciplines in which it has exceptional depth and opportunity—geophysics and climate change, oceanography and fisheries, the clean

45-544 98 - 2

use of fossil fuels, Arctic biology and Arctic engineering, and the economic and social dynamics of the circumpolar north.

S. 660 also envisions that the university will convey to the National Park Service and the U.S. Fish and Wildlife Service thousands of acres of lands that are now inholdings in or adjacent to parks expanded by the 1980 Alaska National Interest Lands Conservation Act. These inholdings will be relinquished to the United States. Thus, the proposed legislation, in addition to making the university whole, would have the added benefit of enhancing the conservation and management of Alaska's vast parks and wilderness areas.

By providing the University of Alaska with a land grant which is both more consistent with what was originally intended and commensurate with the State's size and character, this legislation will permit the University of Alaska to carry out its singular responsibility as a unique and major national center for culture, for learning, and for opportunity in the great far north.

Thank you for permitting this time.

[The prepared statement of Dr. Komisar follows:]

PREPARED STATEMENT OF DR. JEROME B. KOMISAR, PRESIDENT, UNIVERSITY OF ALASKA, FAIRBANKS, AK

Chairman Murkowski and members of the committee. I am Jerome B. Komisar, president of the University of Alaska, a "land-grant university" working in the long tradition of American land-grant universities, providing teaching, research and public service to the people of Alaska. I am here to present the University's views supporting S. 660, the legislation before this committee which would grant federal public lands the University of Alaska and fulfill previous commitments made to it by Congr[illegible]

INTRODUCTION

The University of Alaska is unique among the nation's land-grant colleges. Despite being located in the largest of the 50 states, the University of Alaska has received less than one-third of the land it was legally entitled to receive. As a result, the University has been able to derive only a small portion of the economic benefits that school grant lands were intended to provide.

This constructive inequity is impossible to rationalize for two reasons: first, Alaska's vast size makes possible the devotion of significant acreage to the support of higher education and greater learning; while, second, Alaska's vast distances, its harsh climactic conditions, and the remote locations of many of its cities and villages create prohibitive costs unknown in the rest of the country, which makes such a land grant exemplary public policy. If there is any section of our nation where land grants are necessary to provide essential educational opportunities, it is in the great land of Alaska.

THE HISTORY OF THE UNIVERSITY OF ALASKA'S LAND GRANT

The denial of the University of Alaska's full land grant entitlement is an unintended, yet destructive consequence of the unique circumstances of Alaska's history and entry into the Union. In order to fully understand the need and justification for this legislation, it is first necessary to briefly summarize some of the University's history.

The use of school land grants is a uniquely American innovation. Over the years, as a result of the Morrill Act (including subsequent amendments and related legislation), the system of land grant colleges has continued to grow. Today, there are more than 100 land grant colleges in the United States and in certain U.S. territories and possessions. Collectively, those universities and colleges have received more than 77 million acres of federal lands, from which they have derived millions of dollars to be channeled into higher education.

The University of Alaska has never received federal land grants under the Morrill Act. However, the Territory of Alaska had been provided some school land entitlements through separate legislation. The University of Alaska's story begins in 1915 when the U.S. Congress provided a land grant of approximately 250,000 acres—

every section 33 in the Tanana Valley—to support the Territorial Agricultural College and School of Mines, together with a site for the institution itself.

Unfortunately, the sheer vastness of Alaska—375 million acres—prevented this grant from ever being properly fulfilled. Before they could be reserved for the land grant, the lands had to first be surveyed. As of 1915, only a fraction of one percent of Alaska had been surveyed, virtually none of it in the Tanana Valley. As late as 1952, a mere 0.6 percent of the entire Territory of Alaska had been surveyed. The surveying of land was so slow, indeed, that in 1958 it was estimated it might take up to 1,000 years to fully outline the Territory of Alaska.

The University of Alaska lost a great deal because of the failure to fully survey the Tanana Valley. Ultimately, it was granted only 11,211 acres, or less than 3.3 percent of the approximately 250,000-acre Tanana Valley reservation Congress created for the University's financial support back in 1915. Of the 11,211 acres, about 2,250 acres were the campus site reserved for educational purposes, leaving only 6,961 acres for revenue purposes.

In 1929, another statute granted ". . . for the exclusive use and benefit of the (University) . . ." an additional 100,000 acres of unreserved public lands. Although it was more than 10 years before the University selected any of the 1929 grant, it did eventually select and receive nearly all of the 100,000 acres. Adding this 100,000 to that previously granted, still provided the University with less than one-tenth of one percent of the 375 million acres that make up Alaska. This relative figure places Alaska at the very bottom of the list of land grant colleges. No other State in which there was a land grant for similar purposes received a smaller portion of total state acreage for the support of higher education.

The lack of land was clearly evident in the University's balance sheet. During the first three decades of the University's existence, from 1917 to 1946, the total revenue from land sales, rentals and leases was only $227.90. During that time, the University's land income never amounted to more than $30 a year. Some years were even worse. From 1926 to 1928, Alaska's so-called land-grant college earned only seventy-five cents from its land grant.

Unfortunately, because of federal government inaction in surveying the Territory of Alaska, the University never received the vast majority of the original 1915 land grant. The right to these lands was lost in 1959 because in addition to exempting Alaska from the Morrill Act, the Alaska Statehood Act also repealed Section 1 of the 1915 Alaska School Lands Act. Thus, no further reservations of surveyed land under the 1915 Act could occur.

What land the University did receive was managed by the State, but in an unproductive manner. In 1978, following legislative appropriation of the University's most valuable acreage, the University sued, eventually winning a legislative settlement that reconstituted the University land trust. Later, litigation brought replacement land for the legislatively appropriated acreage. The University's land grant holdings today total 140,000 acres.

Over the last decade, the University has exerted firm management of its lands and has generated over $30,000,000 in revenue. These funds have gone into a Land Grant Trust Fund, established in statute, to provide a perpetual fund to support public postsecondary educational programs for the people of Alaska. The primary use of these earnings is to support basic and applied research in natural resource preservation and development, and in the provision of instructional opportunities throughout the State.

THE STRUCTURE AND SERVICES OF THE UNIVERSITY OF ALASKA

The University of Alaska is the only public institution of higher learning in Alaska. It is a statewide system which consists of three multi-mission universities located in Anchorage, Fairbanks and Juneau with extended satellite colleges and sites throughout the State, including dozens of extension and research sites. The University was established by Congress in 1915 as the Alaska Agricultural College and School of Mines; in 1935, it was renamed the University of Alaska; and in 1959, the year of statehood, it was established as the state university in the Alaska Constitution.

The University has expanded to include full-service universities in Anchorage, Fairbanks and Juneau; lower division college centers in Bethel, Dillingham, Ketchikan, Kodiak, Kotzebue, Nome, Palmer, Sitka and Soldotna; a community college in Valdez; and vocational, rural education and extension sites throughout the State. It is a major American research center in geophysics, oceanography and fisheries, Arctic biology, Northern construction, and mining.

The University is governed by an 11-member Board of Regents, which is appointed by the governor and confirmed by the legislature. I am the chief executive officer for the University system, and chancellors head the major regional instructional units.

The University of Alaska Anchorage offers baccalaureate and associate degrees, as well as certificate programs, through its Colleges of Arts and Sciences, Career and Vocational Education, and Nursing and Health Sciences, as well as the Schools of Business, Education, Engineering and Public Affairs. In addition, master's degrees are offered in nine programs from the campus's colleges and schools. It also provides adult and continuing education programs. Medical science is provided through a joint agreement with the University of Washington. Research programs are emphasized, primarily in biological and health sciences, public policy, and social and economic studies. The College of Community and Continuing Education provides both credit and non-credit instruction to the greater Anchorage area and to all military bases in the State.

The University of Alaska Fairbanks is a comprehensive, four-year, doctoral degree-granting institution with four professional schools and three colleges that offer bachelor's degrees in more than 65 major areas and recognized master's degrees in professional disciplines and doctorates in the sciences and mathematics. The three colleges are the College of Liberal Arts, the College of Sciences, Engineering and Mathematics, and the College of Rural Alaska, with the latter having branch campuses and extended sites throughout the State. The four professional schools consist of the School of Agriculture and Land Resources Management, the School of Mineral Engineering, the School of Management, and the School of Fisheries and Ocean Sciences. These colleges and schools offer certificates, associate and baccalaureate degrees as well as a wide range of technical/vocational programs. Master's degrees are offered in more than 50 fields and doctoral programs are offered in the areas of anthropology, atmospheric sciences, biology, geology, geophysics, mathematics, oceanography, physics, space physics and wildlife management. The University of Alaska Fairbanks is among this nation's 100 leading research universities.

The University of Alaska Southeast is a comprehensive regional university with the primary purpose of providing postsecondary education in Southeast Alaska. The University of Alaska Southeast has campuses in Juneau, Ketchikan and Sitka, and outreach locations throughout its region. It offers certificate programs and associate of applied science degrees in vocational/technical and business-related areas; an associate of arts degree and baccalaureate degrees in the liberal arts, sciences, education, business and public administration; and master's degrees in selected professional fields. In the statewide system, this institution shares responsibility for programs in public administration, early childhood education and educational technology.

The University has an open enrollment policy and will admit into its baccalaureate programs all students with a high school diploma and an overall grade average of 2.0.

Last year, the University of Alaska had a total of nearly 32,000 students, or a full-time equivalent of 16,000 students. More than one in twenty Alaska residents are formally enrolled in credit bearing courses in the University; a figure which does not include the large number of additional residents who benefit from non-credit courses, community development offerings, and applied research in areas of major economic interest. In 1996, we granted 28 doctorates; 421 master's degrees; 1,411 bachelor's degrees; 890 associate degrees and 207 certificates.

BENEFITS TO BE DERIVED FROM COMPLETING THE LAND GRANT

I have described for you, albeit briefly, what the University of Alaska is, and what it does. Now it seems logical to explain how a sufficient land grant would change things. First, even though it may be obvious, I believe I have to state unequivocally that no one is under the impression that a larger grant of land would solve all the University's financial problems immediately. We know better than that, But I believe there are several vital areas of University activity that could be expanded over time with the use of revenue generated by the land.

Prior to 1968, University construction was confined to the original campus at Fairbanks. Following passage of the Alaska Native Land Claims Settlement Act in 1971, and the subsequent formation of village and regional Native corporations, a critical need developed for greater educational opportunities in the rural areas of Alaska was recognized.

The University of Alaska, as the only public institution of higher learning in the State, was expected to expand the delivery of services to rural Alaska and to other urban centers. Many rural and Native leaders felt at the time that the University was not making an adequate response to rural Alaska's special needs. They had a point.

The emphasis turned to building the total university. The Anchorage and Juneau campuses began to expand in the early 1970s and most of the existing community colleges, which had in previous years conducted their programs in public school buildings in the evening and in rented quarters, gained new facilities of their own.

Today, given the concern of rural and Native leaders and the young University's commitment to adjust to changing economic, social and political realities, there is agreement the University continue to fully address the needs of Alaska's rural and Native citizens.

Educational programs for rural Alaska must be developed with special attention to factors which are not usually part of academic program planning, such as building local or cultural relevance into courses, scheduling courses around the living patterns and lifestyles of each rural area, and planning for bilingual instruction if needed.

Alaska's rural and Native students ask only that their learning take place to the greatest extent possible within the physical and philosophical framework of their own communities. No American university has been challenged so greatly. These are communities and villages that do not now have, nor will they have in the foreseeable future, the resources necessary to help the University provide programs and services in their regions.

For more than 20 years now, the University has worked hand-in-hand with rural Alaska, but the vast geographical distance involved makes transportation and communications expensive commodities indeed, and I believe that a sufficient land grant would enable the University to plan more effectively the educational and cultural services needed throughout Alaska.

There are still major economic discrepancies between Natives and non- Natives in Alaska. The percentage of Alaska Natives in the State population is 16 percent, so it is particularly disturbing that the percentage of the Alaska Native work force unemployed consistently hovers around the 20 percent mark, compared to under 10 percent for the rest of Alaska's work force. Rural Alaska has some of the highest unemployment rates in the United States.

The bulk of the professional jobs in rural Alaska, particularly in the fields of health, education and social work are held by non-Native, transient degree-holders, sometimes with little understanding of the culture in which they are working. Rural campuses of the University are putting degrees, licenses and certificates into the hands of local rural residents, including Natives, thus helping to eliminate some of the educational disadvantages that have prevented Natives from taking advantage of professional employment opportunities in Alaska. Most Alaskans who earn degrees in rural Alaska tend to stay in rural Alaska and, degree in hand, land the professional jobs that for decades had most often been filled by imported professionals who stay a few years and then move on.

Clearly, the availability of higher education in remote villages and communities can make a difference in the lives of Alaskans who live in rural areas of the State. There will always be costs attached to the delivery of higher education courses, and the amount of those costs will vary from site to site, depending on a variety of circumstances. The University is committed to utilizing what resources we have in the best possible way for the needs of Alaskans. The fulfillment of the University's land grant would be a significant addition to the University's resources, and I see much of the proceeds from the University's land endowment going into the development of distance delivery programs that would help extend educational opportunities to Alaskans regardless of where they live.

Additional land will enable the University to further the demonstration of exemplary ways of extracting and managing natural resources. It will permit economic development projects and land utilization that balance environmental protection with social progress. The income earned will not only afford the University an opportunity to provide quality instruction to all residents of the State, but to further its research in those disciplines in which it has exceptional depth and opportunity: geophysics and climate change, oceanography and fisheries, the clean use of fossil fuels, arctic biology, and the economic and social dynamics of the circumpolar north.

The legislation your Committee is considering also envisions that the University will eventually convey to the National Park Service and the U.S. Fish and Wildlife Service thousands of acres of University lands that are now inholdings in or adjacent to parks and refuges created or expanded by the 1980 Alaska National Interest Lands Conservation Act. These inholdings would be relinquished to the United States. Thus, the proposed legislation, in addition to making the University whole, would have the added benefit of enhancing the conservation and management of the vast parks, refuges and wilderness areas in Alaska.

By providing the University of Alaska with a land grant which is both more consistent with what was originally intended and commensurate with the State's size and character, this legislation will permit the University of Alaska to carry its singular responsibility as a unique and major national center for culture, for learning, for opportunity in the great far north.

Thank you.

Mr. RENKES. Thank you, Dr. Komisar.

Mr. Tritt, would you like to proceed with your testimony?

STATEMENT OF KEVIN TRITT, PRESIDENT, UNION OF STUDENTS, UNIVERSITY OF ALASKA, ANCHORAGE, AK

Mr. TRITT. Hello. My name is Kevin Tritt. I am the president of the Union of Students at the University of Alaska, Anchorage.

I would like to take this opportunity to thank this committee and Senator Murkowski for raising the issue of the university land grant once again. S. 660 is a very much appreciated effort to provide the University of Alaska with long overdue lands originally promised more than half a century ago.

It has been about 200 years since the first laws were written to set aside lands in support of public education and to provide incentives to develop our newly emerging Nation. Since then many institutions of higher education have been provided a land base from which to build their foundation, provide for their future expansion, and to support academic research. Land grants have also provided many institutions with a viable means of financial support.

But as we approach the dawn of a new millennium, it becomes more apparent that we live in a different age from the days of exploration, expansion, and rapid development of the last 200 years.

Today, we are very aware of the ever-increasing demand for land and the incredible impact that we as humans leave upon the Earth. Public process now provides opportunity for those who wish to get involved to participate at all levels of government. These times call for a re-examination of the purposes, manner, and extent to which land should be conveyed to a university, particularly in Alaska, where development possibilities are seemingly endless and public opinion is so often heated.

The University of Alaska certainly deserves compensation for what was once promised. The real question is, what is the purpose of a university land grant today and does it serve the interests of the public as a whole?

Urban land selections, including Federal surplus lands, are an ideal option for achieving a revenue-generating land base for the university. It is unfortunate that the university's State selection, which would have provided a sizable lease potential within the city of Anchorage, was made available for municipal entitlements, thereby relieving the university of this option. The ensuing settlement with the State provided the university with one-time-only timber rights.

In order to maximize its earning potential, the university has turned to highly controversial clearcutting practices instead of the more environmentally sensitive options of sustainable yield and select cut harvesting. This raises the question of whether the University of Alaska should really be engaged in resource development for the sole purpose of generating revenue.

Both our present Governor, Tony Knowles, and Governor Bill Egan decades before him have vetoed legislation which would have provided a greater land base to the university, citing its failure to address all the factors, including environmental considerations, which should apply to the development of State-held lands. Governor Knowles has additionally expressed the view that it is the State's responsibility to develop its resources and that this responsibility should not be parceled out.

Additionally, making the university dependent upon resource development for its funding compromises the academic foundations of the university and its role as an impartial, objective voice on these sensitive issues in the State. Can the public truly look to the university for guidance on issues of resource development if the institution is actively engaged in aggressively advocating such activity?

It is my understanding that by transferring Federal lands to the university the lands in question would ostensibly become private and would therefore not be held to the same environmental and public process standards warranted by the utilization of a public resource.

I worked as a logger for over 2 years on Eyak land for a company that was ironically dubbed "Sound Development." In that time, I became aware of practices that violated not only a number of laws, including the Alaska Forest Practices Act, but just good common sense. Stream buffers were blatantly ignored and trees were felled regardless of the fact that spawning salmon were literally under foot. I have seen remnants of Forest Service boundaries that were "extended" by fallers to reach a few more choice trees. And while the evidence for these abuses still exists and probably will for decades to come, I have never heard of the developer being held accountable for these alleged violations or even that the charges were being investigated.

When I inquired as to why the State was not monitoring these areas more closely, I was told both that it was private land and that personnel was stretched too thin.

If the university is to become a holder of Federal lands, then any development proposed for these lands should be subject to the full range of public comment as all other Federally or State-held public lands. The reduction of the public process to a maximum of 60 days to comment on the university's tentative land selection is unacceptable. Further, these same lands should be held to all State and Federal environmental regulations that would apply if the land were still held in a true public trust.

National forest lands in the Tongass and Chugach National Forests should be eliminated from the land selection process unless constrained to small-scale research tracts, limited to selective cutting and the promotion of value-added industry. Unless this is the case, the university should not be engaged in timber harvesting at all.

Urban lands, Federal surplus lands, or other selections which would not place the university in a primary resource development role would still provide adequate growth for the university's land base from which to generate revenue. If the University of Alaska is to be a holder of the public's land and trust, then I feel it is our obligation to shine as an example of what the future holds, to explore new ways to live in harmony with our ever-shrinking planet, and be responsible stewards to our future students and the land.

Thank you.

Mr. RENKES. Thank you.

We thank all the witnesses for getting their testimony, their written testimony, in on time, and as a result the chairman has had an opportunity to read everyone's testimony. I know because he has written notes on all of it. So I want to assure you that he has, at least with respect to your written statement—and I think you have all kept to it pretty much—he has had an opportunity to review that, and so what you have done here today is make sure that we get it in the record and the audience here today can also hear you speak.

I apologize again for the situation we are in, but obviously two things have to happen here in the Senate: the committees have to do their business, but the members have to do their work on the floor. And that is controlled by the Majority and Minority Leaders, and they have decided that this would be the process today.

I think, as opposed to—Senator Murkowski waited for the second vote, went over to vote on the first vote at the end of that vote and then waited to vote on the second vote, so he could come back. So what I would like to do maybe is ask, Mr. Fry, rather than have a separate panel, maybe you could come up and you could provide your testimony, if you do not object. Maybe you could provide yours. And Brad Powell, our friend from Ketchikan, if you could provide your testimony now, then we can get that in the record. He has read yours as well, and maybe we can get him back here in time for the questions, as opposed to me starting the questions.

So Mr. Fry, why do not you and Mr. Powell, either one of you.

Mr. Powell, do you have testimony also? No, okay. Mr. Fry, go ahead.

STATEMENT OF TOM FRY, DEPUTY DIRECTOR, BUREAU OF LAND MANAGEMENT, ACCOMPANIED BY BRAD POWELL, FOREST SUPERVISOR, TONGASS NATIONAL FOREST, KETCHIKAN DISTRICT, ALASKA

Mr. FRY. Well, let me introduce Mr. Powell, who is the Forest Supervisor for the Tongass in the Ketchikan District. He is here as the representative not only of the area, but also as the representative of the Department of Agriculture.

Mr. Chairman, I appreciate the opportunity to be able to speak to you today about S. 660 and to participate on such a distinguished panel. I would like to ask, if appropriate now, that my written remarks be made a part of the record.

Mr. RENKES. Yes, your written remarks will be incorporated into the record.

Mr. FRY. I will very quickly summarize my remarks, which I think were fairly short in the first place and also are somewhat duplicative of some of the remarks that have already been made.

As you are well aware, this administration strongly supports education and educational efforts. However, the issues raised in this bill we think relate to whether or not the Federal Government has fulfilled its obligations and responsibilities to the State of Alaska in terms of land and land grants.

In the invitation that we received to participate in this hearing, you asked that we look at the legislative history or the legislation that has preceded this legislation today. So very briefly, and it has already been outlined by a number of the witnesses, let me just touch on two or three points.

In the 1800's the Morrill Act was passed, which created an opportunity for funding for land grant colleges.

The CHAIRMAN. Go ahead and proceed, Tom.

Mr. FRY. Thank you, Mr. Chairman.

In 1915, a bill was passed which was passed in order to support schools within the State of Alaska which set aside each section 33 surveyed in the Tanana Valley. Alaska ultimately was able to select and receive over 11,000 acres from that bill.

In 1929, another bill was passed dealing with some of the problems that were created by the 1915 Act. The 1915 Act, as was mentioned earlier, required for a number of surveys to take place and those surveys were going very slowly. So the 1929 Act was passed and authorized that in lieu of lands that had not been taken by the 1915 bill, 100,000 acres of land be granted to the State for the use by the university.

In 1958, the Statehood Act was passed. In that act there were grants that were made for internal improvements. Those internal improvements of that act included schools and school lands. What the act did was consolidate all of the internal improvement provisions of State grants and consolidated them into one grant of 102-plus million acres.

Again, the issue came up in 1980 when the Congress passed ANILCA. They were still concerned that the State schools had not received their fair share based on lands that they had not received in the 1915 Act. So ANILCA granted an additional 75,000 acres for schools and attempted to settle any disputes that were created by the 1958 Statehood Act or the 1915 Act that granted specific lands to the schools.

So Mr. Chairman, the Federal Government feels that it has fully discharged its responsibilities to the State of Alaska and provided four times more land for the State than provided for any other State. If passed by the Congress, the Secretary of Agriculture and the Secretary of the Interior will recommend that the President veto this bill.

I look forward to any questions, Mr. Chairman.

[The prepared statement of Mr. Fry follows:]

PREPARED STATEMENT OF TOM FRY, DEPUTY DIRECTOR, BUREAU OF LAND MANAGEMENT

Mr. Chairman and members of the committee, thank you for the opportunity to testify on S. 660, which would direct the Secretary to convey a minimum of 250,000 acres of Federal lands to the University of Alaska. S. 660 further directs the Secretary to convey additional acreage, up to 250,000 acres, if the State were to convey an equal amount. Pursuant to the terms of the bill, the University would be able to choose some of the most valuable 500,000 acres of Federal land in the State. Unlike nearly all other statutes disposing of public land, there is no requirement in S. 660 that lands be vacant, unreserved, or unappropriated. This bill would allow the University to select lands from the National Petroleum Reserve-Alaska, the Tongass National Forest, or other areas of great value to the citizens of the United States.

Because the United States has fully discharged its responsibilities to the State of Alaska with regard to the university lands entitlement and the impact on sensitive Federal lands could be profound, the Secretary of the Department of the Interior and the Secretary of the Department of Agriculture strongly oppose this bill and will recommend a veto if it passes the Congress.

LEGISLATION TO COMPENSATE ALASKA FOR THE ORIGINAL SCHOOL LAND GRANT

The underlying premise of this bill is faulty. The bill presumes that the University of Alaska never received the quantity of land that Congress intended to bestow upon it. It implies that the Federal government failed to provide an adequate land base, and as a result the University has failed to achieve its full potential.

Contrary to the claims asserted in S. 660, Congress has already enacted legislation to fully compensate Alaska for original university land grants.

The Act of March 4, 1915, set aside each surveyed section 33 in the Tanana Valley for the support of a Territorial agricultural college. Twenty-six of these sections were surveyed and 11,850.60 acres were transferred to the Territory for the benefit of an agricultural college and school of mines.

On January 21, 1929, while survey and transfer under the Act of March 4, 1915, was ongoing, Congress provided an additional 100,000-acre grant to the Territory on behalf of the University. The 1929 Act did not restrict the land grants to sections in place, but instead allowed Alaska to select vacant, unappropriated, and unreserved land anywhere within the Territory's boundaries. This gave the Territory the opportunity to choose the highest value land from all lands meeting the selection criteria. To date, 99,417 acres of this grant have been transferred to the State.

The Act of March 4, 1915 was repealed by the Alaska Statehood Act in 1959, although the sections that had already been surveyed continued to be reserved for future conveyance to the State. There was a lingering dispute in 1980 between Alaska and the Federal government concerning which land grant sections vested in the State at the time of Statehood and which sections were revoked in the Alaska Statehood Act. To resolve this, Congress passed section 906(b) of the Alaska National Interest Lands Conservation Act, granting the State 75,000 acres of land and clearly stating that any and all Federal obligations under the Act of March 4, 1915, had been extinguished. Section 906(b) states that:

> In full and final settlement of any and all claims by the State of Alaska arising under the Act of March 4, 1915 . . . as confirmed and transferred in section 6(k) of the Alaska Statehood Act, the State is hereby granted seventy-five thousand acres which it shall be entitled to select until January 4, 1994, from vacant, unappropriated, and unreserved public lands. In exercising the selection rights granted herein, the State shall be deemed to have relinquished all claims to any right, title, or interest to any school lands which failed to vest under the above statutes at the time Alaska became a State (January 3, 1959), including lands unsurveyed on that date or surveyed lands which were within Federal reservations or withdrawals on that date.

THE ALASKA STATEHOOD ACT

In the Alaska Statehood Act, Congress rejected the previous methods used to provide for state institutions (i.e., making specific sections available or setting aside specific acreage for categories of state institutions). Congress opted instead to give the new state a general purpose land grant of 102,550,000 acres. This provided Alaska with the needed flexibility to chart its own course. Subsequent decisions made by the State concerning the funding of its university system were to be freely made in Alaska, by Alaskans.

Alaska was never short-changed in the amount of land it received to support its university system. The original land grant formula to states in support of higher education is known as the Morrill Act. The amount of land awarded each state under the Morrill Act was based on the state's population, not its size. Had Alaska been a state in 1862 when the original Morrill Act passed, it would have received a total of 90,000 acres (30,000 acres each for one Representative and two Senators). Although Alaska was not a state and did not fall under the purview of the Morrill Act, it actually received more land through the Act of March 4, 1915, and the Act of January 21, 1929, described above.

Section 6(l) of the Alaska Statehood Act explicitly states that Alaska will not be entitled to receive any additional lands under the Morrill Act, making it clear that Congress did not overlook the university in the Statehood Act, but concluded that it had adequately provided for the needs of all State institutions through the general purpose grant of 102.5 million acres in Section 6(b).

The responsibility for providing the remaining land endowment for the Alaska university system clearly passed to the State of Alaska with passage of the Alaska Statehood Act. Congress made it clear that in giving the State a land entitlement of 102.5 million acres, it was extinguishing and fully satisfying previous university land entitlements. In other words, Alaska was given a block land grant with a proviso that the grant was "in lieu" of previous and future grants for internal improvement.

The specific Alaska Statehood bills passed by the houses of Congress addressed the "in lieu" issue. Those bills were H.R. 7999 and S. 49. H.R. 7999 read as follows:

> The grants provided for in this Act shall be in lieu of the grant of land (emphasis added) for purposes of internal improvements made to new States by section 8 of the Act of September 4, 1841, (5 Stat. 455), and sections 2378 and 2379 of the Revised Statutes (43 U.S.C. sec. 857), and in lieu of the swampland grant made by the Act of September 28, 1850, (9 Stat. 520), and section 2479 of the Revised Statutes (43 U.S.C. sec. 982), and in lieu of the grant of thirty thousand acres for each Senator and Representative in Congress made by the Act of July 2, 1862, as amended (12 Stat. 503; 7 U.S.C., secs. 301-308 [The Morrill Act]), which grants are hereby declared not to extend to the State of Alaska.

S. 49 provided for a general grant of 102,550,000 acres and an "in lieu" subsection which was identical to H.R. 7999 above.

Due to differences in the two bills, conferees met and agreed upon H.R. 7999 with certain concessions to S. 49, including a quantity grant of 102,500,000 acres. Both houses passed the bill as amended by the conferees. The final version, as reflected by section 6(b) of the Alaska Statehood Act, provided a quantity land grant of 102,550,000 acres with only a very few internal improvement grants, namely: 6(a) for community expansion; 6(c) and 6(d) for government buildings in Juneau; and 6(e) for improvements used in fish and wildlife conservation and protection.

Congress intended the larger quantity land grant to expunge any federal responsibility for any specialized internal improvements grants such as to the University of Alaska. The tenor of both the House and Senate versions of the statehood bills was that the State of Alaska would be responsible for deciding for itself which internal improvements to undertake, and how generously or penuriously to provide for those internal improvements.

S. 660 must be rejected because it is entirely inconsistent with the legislation and legislative histories discussed in this testimony.

COSTS TO THE AMERICAN TAXPAYERS UNDER THIS LEGISLATION

As previously stated, S. 660 allows the University to select lands of tremendous value to the American taxpayers. The proposed legislation provides no exceptions for the high value lands held by the American taxpayers, such as the Tongass National Forest, the pipeline corridor, the National Petroleum Reserve-Alaska, and offshore interests. Similarly, there is no protection for areas with unique values like the Steese National Conservation Area or the White Mountains National Recreation Area.

Depending upon the tracts selected, the costs of the proposed legislation in terms of future lost revenue to the Federal treasury could be significant. Onshore and offshore leasable minerals could be selected. It is also likely that the University would pursue multiple tracts of high value timber from the Tongass National Forest, the United States' premier temperate rain forest located in southeastern Alaska. The effect could be to fatally undermine the Tongass National Forest Land Use Management Plan and require a new plan.

In addition to lost revenue and planning costs, the survey, adjudication and management costs of the proposal could be significant.

CONCLUSION

At Statehood, the Congress provided Alaska with 102.5 million acres of land, more than four times the amount of Federal land provided to any other state, in part to provide land for higher education. Subsequent decisions made by the State concerning the allocation of lands for the university system were freely made in Alaska, by Alaskans. The United States has fully discharged its responsibilities. It is clearly not appropriate for the United States to provide additional public lands to the State of Alaska for an entitlement that has been fully satisfied.

Mr. Chairman, that concludes my prepared remarks. Thank you again for the opportunity to testify on S. 660. I am now prepared to respond to any questions you may have.

The CHAIRMAN. You know, I find it kind of frustrating, I guess as an Alaskan, the fact that the administration takes a position on a veto threat prior to the hearing process. I would like to think that the hearing process would have some effect on enlightening and providing information and background. But it seems like this particular administration has a policy of proceeding on the basis of hardly less than a public process, which I find an extraordinary inconsistency because they pride themselves on the public process and the hearing process and the input of the people. Yet they have no hesitation to come up prior to the process with a preconceived threat of a veto. I think that is a bit irresponsible, and you can pass that on to the powers that be.

Mr. FRY. I will take that back.

The CHAIRMAN. And you can even ad lib a little bit, if you are so inclined, to the rationale that I have thrown back at you, that they pride themselves on the public process. I do not know where the press is in picking it up and calling their bluff, but I do not have any problem seeing through it.

Have you had any extended conversations with the State administration about the equity of the State of Alaska, the University of Alaska's, a land grant college, and the situation the university is in, virtually no land, the largest State? Next to the State of Delaware, in looking at that chart over there, and we have got a smaller version of it that I can see easier sitting around here somewhere: New Mexico, 1.3 million acres; Oklahoma, a little over a million acres; New York, 980,000, something like that.

Have you had any conversations with the State administration?

Mr. FRY. I have not, sir.

The CHAIRMAN. Have any of your folks, to your knowledge?

Mr. FRY. Not to my knowledge.

The CHAIRMAN. And yet that would be the correct agency? In other words, you assume that a significant amount of any acreage would come out of BLM?

Mr. FRY. I think, the way this act is written, Mr. Chairman, acreage could come from places such as the Federal offshore, it could come from NPRA, which is BLM land, it could also come from national forests, which is Department of Agriculture.

The CHAIRMAN. Now, is there anything in the legislation as you read it that would direct where it comes from?

Mr. FRY. Other than the specific exclusions that are set out, no.

The CHAIRMAN. It would not come from parks, it would not come from wilderness areas.

Mr. FRY. That is right.

The CHAIRMAN. It would not come from where else? Wildlife refuges?

Mr. FRY. That is right. Conservation areas.

The CHAIRMAN. It could come from every place else.

Mr. FRY. That is my understanding.

The CHAIRMAN. You know, I am surprised out there, because I have read some of the testimony and there is a presumption that it is going to come from X, Y, and Z specifically, and the testimony is extensive, whether it be the Naval Petroleum Reserve Alaska, whether it be the Tongass, and the threats and potentials and so forth.

You know, what I also find is extraordinary is the board of regents, a group of Alaskans, pretty knowledgeable and respected group appointed by the Governor, subject to confirmation, I believe, by the State legislature—is that correct, Dr. Komisar?

Dr. KOMISAR. Yes.

The CHAIRMAN. And to suggest that somehow this group, regardless of where this land is ultimately selected, is going to act irresponsibly on behalf of Alaskans, when they are accountable for the land selections to the Governor and accountable to the State legislature, I find that very inconsistent, any more than taking your delegation, your elected delegation. You know, we are accountable. We have to vote yes or no.

But there is among the opponents of this an extraordinary generalization that somehow, if the university is successful in selecting this land, it is going to be an irresponsible action by Alaskans. What an extraordinary extension and lack of confidence.

You know, for those of you who are opposed to any development on any land, which you are, and the shoe can fit, this is the only time when this delegation happens to be in a position of committee chairmanships of appropriate jurisdiction, that we can get these things done. We will not be able to get them done.

So I am going to go back and vote and Gregg is going to take over the balance of this hearing, and I am going to come back, because we were successful, evidently, in negotiating a tradeoff. The tradeoff, of course, involved an objection by the minority of the U.S. Senate against holding hearings past 2 hours. So I promptly put a hold on all their nominations. So they have agreed now to allow us to continue hearings uninterrupted throughout the month, and I have agreed to let their nominations go.

Mr. Renkes.

Mr. RENKES. Well, as you can tell, it is a tense morning over in the U.S. Senate, but then the political process would not work without tension.

He would like to continue his question, the chairman would, and so he is going to vote on these two votes and then come back as soon as he can. So in the interim, I think I will proceed with a few questions from his list.

Mr. Koehler, if this legislation had excluded or would exclude national forests from those lands available for the university to select from, would you support or your group support the bill?

Mr. KOEHLER. I think we would note that it would be an improvement, but I do not believe we could support the bill, because we have problems with the very premise of getting more land from the Federal Government.

Mr. RENKES. Okay.

Mr. KOEHLER. I am sorry Senator Murkowski had to leave after his remarks, because I was going to try to engage him in a little discussion.

Mr. RENKES. I think you will have a chance when he comes back, so if you can just hold that.

Mr. KOEHLER. Thanks for your question.

Mr. RENKES. Mr. Tritt, are you willing to—you expressed some concern about the position the university's been put in to manage lands for resource development in order to help fund the university. I think your observations about the municipal land that the university at one time had an opportunity to use and the fact that the

State had worked out a deal where they were basically directed toward timber harvesting were pretty accurate, and I commend you for a well thought out statement.

You also expressed concern about the public process and the fact that private lands are not subject to the same type of public process that public lands are subject to. Obviously, Senator Murkowski has pointed out that the board of regents is a somewhat public group in the sense that the members are appointed by the Governor and confirmed by the legislature, therefore have some public responsibilities. The university itself is in some senses a public organization, and as a landholder it is not necessarily a private landholder. It has public functions and responsibilities that are probably different than the average private landholder.

So, given that, would you be willing to work with the board of regents and the officials of the university to try to make this a better bill? Because there are certainly things—we have not talked to them about this, but there are certainly things that they can do in establishing guidelines and public processes of their own with respect to resource development.

I am just wondering if that is something you have thought about and if that is something you are willing to engage in.

Mr. TRITT. I would love to undertake that with the board of regents and the administration. In regards to the policy that the regents already have completed, I believe the drafts of their land management plans have already been completed, and I can make sure that your office receives some of those, copies of those.

They are comforting, to see that they are heading in that direction. When I addressed the issue of public process and meeting all State and/or Federal requirements regarding the environment, it came from a position of basically do not trust anybody. If this is a piece of legislation that is going to be going through, then why not just say it right out, get that out of the way so that you do not have to leave it for somebody else to decide and basically keep the fight up?

There is also—I also have some concern sometimes with attitudes by certain members of our regents who do not share the same concern for the environment and the process that I do and a lot of my fellow students do. But I do definitely believe that the regents have started movements in the right direction as far as laying out their policies, which will ensure that certain public processes are met and that their land selections meet what is best for the university.

But at the same time, we are in a position where we are losing State revenue and in order to support the university's mission it is going to be very important to find alternatives sources. I do not want to see the university put in a position where they may be hesitant, but nonetheless want to select certain undesirable resource development lands simply because they need the money. That is a possibility here, and I would prefer to see that not be a viable option.

Mr. RENKES. Dr. Komisar, is the university willing to consider alternatives or changes to the legislation that either in regard to the lands that would be selected or available for selection or in terms of the public process or the land planning process or public involvement, to improve this bill from the perception of some of the detractors? Would you be willing to engage in that kind of discussion of proposed changes to the legislation?

Dr. KOMISAR. Very much so. The university's interest is in stabilizing a future income stream, and it is important to the university that it has processes for selection that not only allow the public an opportunity to speak to the university, but allows the university an opportunity to understand the public mood.

The land grant will never provide 100 percent of the university's necessary income and our relationship to the public is always going to be very important. So we are willing to work with all groups that are interested in this and certainly look forward to improving the bill.

Mr. RENKES. In Mr. Koehler's testimony he referred to the original basis on which land was provided to land grant universities, which appeared to be population. In fact, it may have been tied to the number of representatives that particular State had in Congress at that time. He correctly points out that Alaska's population puts it at about 48th, 49th among the number of States.

Mr. KOEHLER. Wyoming.

Mr. RENKES. Wyoming, yes. Mr. Koehler is very familiar with Wyoming. He likes unpopulated States.

Anyway, my point was that, even though the original basis was population, in fact universities have developed different roles over the years. The University of Alaska serves far more than the resident Alaska population's educational needs. I was wondering if you could speak to the national, international role that the University of Alaska has taken on and why these types of revenues are important to continuing those efforts.

Dr. KOMISAR. The original distribution under the Morrill Act was by population and it was based upon representation in Congress. I think it was 30,000 acres per representative in Congress. It was done at a time period that ended up with the law being much more effective in the northeastern United States than elsewhere in the United States, and if you were going to go through the same process today you would have a much different kind of distribution of acreage taking place.

The fact that it was biased toward certain sections of the country where indeed land values were much higher because of the density of population created an unfairness in the process, which is something Congress has corrected on occasion. That is the only way you have New Mexico and Oklahoma having over a million acres each, is that there was a departure from the original Morrill Act formulation on this.

Indeed, the University of Alaska not only works with the population of the State, but is an international center in science and a major international center for trade in the northern Pacific.

Mr. MALNAK. Dr. Komisar, one of the other things we heard about is that the university actually has about 140,000 acres of land, yet there is a Federal grant of somewhere between 100 or 111,000 acres. Can you explain the difference between maybe the 112,000 acres and the 140? It has been suggested they have been given up to 180 at some points.

Dr. KOMISAR. I do not think I can give you a complete explanation of it, but much of the original 112 was appropriated by the legislature. And then there were a number of lawsuits, and I think at the end of the legal process it ended up with 140,000 acres. But the amount that was actually given by Congress was the 112,000 figure. It was only because of legal issues that arose and an attempt to make the original land grant whole that you ended up with a larger amount.

Mr. RENKES. Dr. Komisar, does the university's board of regents support this legislation?

Dr. KOMISAR. Very much so. They have been in support of it all along, very strong support.

Mr. RENKES. If you could tell us a little bit about the kind of dialogue that has gone into considering this legislation over a long period of time and how the board of regents came to their position?

Dr. KOMISAR. The university as early as the creation of statehood was interested in making certain that it would get what it considered the full commitment that had been made by the Federal Government. So as early as 1959 there was discussion of a land grant and that has continued until today.

But, this has been talked about under a number of different university administrations and I think began perhaps during my stay, I think, during the second year that I was president of the university, about 6 years ago. The board has given a lot of intense consideration to this and a deep feeling of two things: one, that there was a commitment that they would like to see made whole; and two, that a land grant would just be essential to the future of the university. That is perhaps the only way to guarantee the kind of stability that a higher education organization needs in this day and age.

Mr. RENKES. Governor Knowles in his statement for the record expressed concern about the university selecting lands within the NPRA because he feels that potentially this would deprive the State of its share of mineral leasing revenues. I wonder if you have any comment on that.

Dr. KOMISAR. I think under the current law, NPRA land, if it was to be developed and there was income the government from that, it would be split between the Federal Government and the State government on a 50-50 basis. So I am sort of surprised by that position, since the university is an entity of the State and we would be getting 100 percent of the income for what is one of the most important State functions and State purposes.

Mr. RENKES. Mr. Koehler, the legislation—Senator Murkowski was pointing out that the legislation does not target any particular area of the State. Wilderness areas, national monuments within the national forest system and outside, wildlife refuges, wild and scenic rivers, and parks are excluded from selection. Why do you not have confidence in the board of regents to make appropriate selections for this particular land entitlement, this 250,000 acres? Why do you lack confidence in the board of regents to basically do the right thing, represent Alaskans, not pick particularly—you have listed in your testimony some environmentally sensitive areas that in 1990, after careful consideration, Congress set aside from resource development.

Why would the board of regents choose those areas at this juncture and attempt to develop those areas?

Mr. KOEHLER. Let me explain our concern, Gregg. It is that, the way the legislation is written, it does not prohibit selection of those what are known as legislated LUD II's in the jargon, those areas that were set aside by the Tongass Timber Reform Act that are not technically conservation system units under the Alaska Lands Act.

That is a deep concern for not only our organization, but other organizations and many, many small communities in southeastern Alaska, because everywhere they look is the Tongass National Forest, whether it is their front yard or their back yard or the watershed they depend on for their fisheries. And many of those areas were set aside as those LUD II's, and as the bill is written those areas could be selected.

Mr. RENKES. But why would they be selected by the board of regents?

Mr. KOEHLER. Well, I think some members on the board of regents that are on there that were appointed by Governor Hickel or others would very much like to try to get a hold of those lands in the legislated LUD II's, and if that did not work then go for some lands on the Tongass. That is our view on it.

We think it would be a lot simpler just to eliminate the temptation to select any national forest lands, period. I think that the university has to act responsibly, the board of regents has to act responsibly. But they have done things that the current Governor does not agree with, particularly the selection of lands in the Brady Glacier or the proposal to pick up some lands there in the Glacier National Park. That is a whole other issue, but I know there is a huge disagreement between the Governor and the board of regents on that decision.

So we would feel much better if the legislation was drafted much more carefully and deliberately to eliminate as many problems as possible. So if somehow—we do not support the premise that the university should get any more lands, but if somehow that was decided, that those decisions could be made in a way without a lot of controversy, and I think that would probably help the university out as well.

Mr. RENKES. Dr. Komisar, there has been a lot of—there has been concern expressed about the ability of the university to properly manage its lands, and there has been some references made to the situation at Icey Bay and Yakataga. Can you address that situation and kind of flesh that out a little bit?

Dr. KOMISAR. I would be happy to. The university over the last 10 years I think has been very successful in terms of the management of its land. Prior to that time period there was a relatively loose management, but I think it has been a tight management since then and a forward management since then.

The land at Icey Bay is not owned by the university. What the university acquired down there was the rights to a single harvest of the timber. So that the fiduciary responsibility of the board had to be exercised through a process of selling and cutting wood, and that is what was done and was done I think within, I know within the standards of the timber industry, within the high standards of the timber industry.

Mr. KOEHLER. Gregg, could I just add a point here?

Mr. RENKES. Sure.

Mr. KOEHLER. In our written comments you will notice—I wish the copies were a little better, but—photographs of recent clear-cutting operations that have taken place for the university, including one that is near Slide Ridge outside of Ketchikan. Some people who have visited Ketchikan will see that. I think that cut was done 5 or 6 years ago. The logging on Yakataga has been really extensive and pretty legendary as far as really bad forest practices.

I think the other concern you might see—recently we saw some things in the newspaper, the last piece on our testimony, about the university selling off waterfront, scenic view and remote properties. "Own a piece of the last frontier," it says, and there is a whole huge ad in there. If lands are to be held in a public trust, we do not think that is the way to manage them, at least the current track record.

Thank you.

[Pause.]

Mr. RENKES. Mr. Fry, you mentioned legislation passed in 1915 setting aside every section 33 in the Tanana Valley for the university. If this was done, the university would have received approximately 250,000 acres from the Federal Government. The reason this was not done is because the Federal Government, actually the BLM, did not survey the land in time.

Does the Department of the Interior shoulder no responsibility in light of the fact that the BLM's ineffectiveness in the early part of this century is partly to blame for the university's dilemma today?

Mr. FRY. Well, I can assure you that none of us were there to know what was going on.

Mr. RENKES. Right. That is why I changed it to the BLM.

Mr. FRY. My understanding of surveying in Alaska is that it may be some of the most difficult surveying in the entire United States. As you are well aware, we have a number of things that we are involved in in BLM that involve surveying, trying to pick up a lot of different lands that have been selected by Native corporations, individual allotments, and that surveying process is the largest that we have in the Bureau. It continues to move forward, but the difficulties of surveying Alaska are legendary.

Whether or not we want to call that blame or call it a fact of life, I do not know. But it is absolutely true that that was not the way to go. I think that is what the Congress recognized in 1929 when they backed away from that section selection and went to the more general selection of 100,000 acres.

Mr. RENKES. Thank you.

You mentioned that 75,000 acres was granted to the State in ANILCA. Was this land reserved for the university?

Mr. FRY. It is my understanding that it went for both the university, and schools within Alaska. But I would rather submit something directly, provide something for the record to specifically answer that question, because I am not sure.

Mr. RENKES. Okay. Thank you.

Mr. FRY. Unless someone else has something.

[The information referred to follows:]

The 75,000 acres granted by Section 906(b) of Alaska National Interest Lands Conservation Act (ANILCA) was for both the University and schools in Alaska. History of Section 906(b):

In 1976, discussions were undertaken between representatives of the Department of the Interior and the State of Alaska to dispose of any claims by the State of Alaska concerning surviving rights by school lands or University lands as those categories of lands were incorporated into the Alaska Statehood Act. Section 906(b) of ANILCA resulted from those discussions. From 1978 through the final passage of ANILCA, this section received no major amendments nor did anyone ever feel the necessity for an in-depth discussion of the purport of section 906(b). It was always referred to and explained in a very abbreviated manner.

Section 906(b) expressly states:

> (1) In full and final settlement of any and all claims by the State of Alaska arising under the Act of March 4, 1915 (38 Stat. 1214)

43 U.S.C. 1635(b).

A copy of that statute is here attached for your convenience. That statute included grants for the public school system and for the University. Both institutions are schools, collectively these land grants can be referred to as "school lands," in turn, in the Alaska Statehood Act, the right to these lands were transferred to the new State of Alaska. Section 906(b) of ANILCA expressly states that it is in settlement of all claims arising from the 1915 Act. Most of the disputes that have arisen concerned the land grant portion of the public school grant. Nevertheless, the words of section 906(b) clearly encompass a settlement of any dispute relating to either the University or the public schools.

On August 19, 1980, in an exchange on the floor of the Senate, Senator Stevens and Senator Jackson clearly established that school lands, university lands, and state lands are all encompassed in the concept of "state lands" in the language of Title IX of ANILCA. The appropriate quotes are as follows:

Mr. STEVENS. There has been some question raised as to whether lands conveyed to the State of Alaska under the university, school land and mental health grants are State lands under the definition of the Statehood Act and this act. I would like to clarify that these lands are State lands and are subject to the same protection and status of any lands conveyed under the Alaska Statehood Act.

Mr. JACKSON. The Senator is correct. We clearly intended at the passage of the Alaska Statehood Act that such lands conveyed to the State of Alaska or its political subdivisions, including the University of Alaska, would be considered State lands for purposes of Federal law. This bill reaffirms that status of these lands.

126 Cong. Rec. S. 11196 (August 19, 1980).

The Department of the Interior believes that Section 6 of the Alaska Statehood Act satisfied any obligations of the United States to the University of Alaska. The final settlement set out in section 906(b) of ANILCA is only incidental to the conclusion that the University has no further claims against the United States. An interpretation of section 906(b) is not critical to the conclusion that the University has no further claims. However, it is clear that the University has no enforceable claims arising out of the Act of March 4, 1915.

Mr. KOEHLER. Can I comment on that? I think it is a question—when we came upon this section of ANILCA we were surprised, first of all, because it was a fairly unknown section. And it does refer to "school land settlement," which opens the question whether that was for schools or whether that was for the university. I will grant that that question is probably out there.

The thing that catches our interest in it is because the next phrase in the law talks about "a full and final settlement of any and all claims by the State of Alaska arising under the Act of March 4, 1915," which is the one that granted the Tanana Valley lands, the 250,000 acres. So that extinguished that claim. So it is our belief that there is a definite reference to university lands, that those lands could have been utilized by the university, and I have a serious question on what happened to those lands.

Mr. RENKES. Well, the lands were not granted to the university, were they?

Mr. KOEHLER. But they were granted to the State of Alaska.

Mr. RENKES. But not to the university.

Mr. KOEHLER. The State of Alaska could have utilized them for the university. So I have been asking in all honesty the question of where did those 75,000 acres go.

Mr. KOEHLER. Dr. Komisar, do you want to comment on that?

Dr. KOMISAR. It might be good to get a complete answer from Tom Fry, but as I understand it the 1915 legislation had lands for schools and then land for the university, that they were two different sections. And what the 75,000 acres did was handle the school issue, but not the one of the university land grant.

Mr. KOEHLER. If I may add, it clearly extinguished—it was a full and final settlement of any and all claims under that act, which would include the university claims. So it said, we have given enough, as Mr. Fry had said earlier.

Mr. RENKES. Mr. Fry, can you point to specific language in the Statehood Act that dedicated land to the university and how much land that was?

Mr. FRY. I do not think that there is a specific designation of any land to the university. I think it takes a little look at history. If you look back at the Morrill Act, of course, that was the 30,000 for each Congressman and Senator. Then as States started coming into the Union in the 1900's, specifically States like New Mexico and Arizona, Congress started making grants in lieu of the Morrill Act, and in those particular grants they tended to list: 500,000 acres for a university, a certain number of acres for prisons, on and on and on and on.

What is different about the Alaska Act is that the Alaska Act consolidated into one package all of those internal improvement provisions and specifically mentions the internal improvements, specifically mentions in the act in section 6(l) the fact that this extinguishes or is in lieu of land that would have been granted under the Morrill Act, both 1841 and 1862.

So it is dealing with the question of lands and for all the internal improvements, including the university. But there is no specific grant. This was one of those situations—being from Texas, we kind of like to handle our own destiny. I think Alaskans are much the same way, and I think in this particular situation Alaska wanted to get the total grant and take that grant and use it as it saw fit to take care of all of those internal improvements.

Mr. RENKES. Are you aware of any other State that has given a portion of the lands that it received from the Federal Government to its Federal land grant college?

Mr. FRY. I have to ask you to ask that question again.

Mr. RENKES. Are you aware of any other State that has given a portion of the lands that it received from the Federal Government to its Federal land grant college?

Mr. FRY. As I mentioned, like in the case of New Mexico and Arizona, when they came into statehood there were specific grants in those statutes for those particular provisions, for those particular purposes.

Mr. RENKES. The grants were to the university, not to the State.

Mr. FRY. I think they came through the State to the university, but it was specifically designated as to where those would go.

Mr. RENKES. Right, and that specificity is lacking in the Alaska Statehood Act?

Mr. FRY. Absolutely.

Mr. RENKES. The Statehood Act also had some language that referred to the revenues that the State of Alaska would achieve from the Federal lands. Ninety percent of the mineral revenues from the Federal lands would go to the State of Alaska. And there is some reference to that as a compensating factor in the grant of land to the State.

But the 1980 Act set a number of, a large portion of those lands and resources, off limits to mineral development, so in some sense trumped that original assumption that the State would have these resources available to it. So do you think that this changed at all the value of the grant of land to the State of Alaska?

Mr. FRY. I think the State of Alaska, had they so chosen, could have still made substantial grants to the universities and, to the extent the universities had not been made whole, the State could have made them whole.

Mr. RENKES. Thank you.

Dr. Komisar, what kinds of activities do you foresee the university undertaking with the land grant?

Dr. KOMISAR. There is a whole range of activities. Are you looking at the activities that we would support with the income from the land grant?

Mr. RENKES. Well, maybe if you could answer both questions: What kinds of development activities is the university most interested in engaging in at this time; and then what kinds of—how would these revenues—you have mentioned stability and certainty for the university, but what are some of the needs of the university at this time?

Dr. KOMISAR. Going to the concept of land selection and what would be the kind of economic development that we would want, I think the discussions within the university are at a preliminary level, and we would go through really a process that would look at two things: first, the availability of land in different areas of the State; and second, what the likelihood was of development and what the contributions, potential contributions, could be from that source of development.

We would expect to be working closely with the natural resource industries in trying to get as much information from all groups in the State before going through a selection process.

When it comes to the use of the income from the land grant, that would be very diverse and very, very widespread. But of great significance would be to handle some of the areas that are very expensive at the University of Alaska, which is really delivering educational services around the vast land mass, that it is very expensive to deliver educational services in remote areas of Alaska or to connect the cities together. So there would be a large investment in the educational infrastructure of the program.

There also would be an investment in those areas where we have considerable research ability. Fisheries and oceanography would be a strong one; Arctic biology would be another; natural mineral development would be another. So there is just a lot of activities.

Then there is the general day to day costs that the university has to meet in educating its students.

Mr. RENKES. This bill would provide an opportunity for the university to transfer back inholdings that it currently holds in Federal lands. Can you discuss those inholdings?

Dr. KOMISAR. We have—I do not have a list of the inholdings in front of me right now.

Mr. RENKES. We have a chart.

Dr. KOMISAR. Oh, you have one. You just put a chart right up there.

We have inholdings in a number of national wildlife refuge areas, in Wrangell-St. Elias National Park and Preserve, in Denali National Park, Kenai Fjord National Park. And it is those inholdings that we are talking about trading in for different land.

Mr. RENKES. Mr. Fry, do you know, is there interest in the part of the Department of the Interior, not speaking for the Park Service but in the Department of the Interior, in these inholdings?

Mr. FRY. I have never participated in a discussion on these particular inholdings, but we are oftentimes interested in consolidating lands within parks and refuges that may have inholdings.

Mr. RENKES. Thank you.

The CHAIRMAN. I apologize for the inconvenience, but I hope you were not inconvenienced. Thank you, Gregg, and thank you, Brian.

I guess I left with the thought that if you cannot trust the board of regents to make decisions that are right—they are really not much different than any other elected official that has to be held accountable to make decisions that are right.

Mr. Tritt, you are a member of that board as the student body—you are not a member of the board, but you are the student body president and as a consequence you sit with the board, is that correct?

Mr. TRITT. I attend their meetings and participate on a regular basis.

The CHAIRMAN. And you participate. What is your assessment of the qualifications of the board relative to their dedication and commitment to the university?

Mr. TRITT. Oh, I think they are very committed to the university, and I think we have a very diverse and respected board. But the concern that I might raise is that there are a couple of our board members who are particularly interested in developing natural resources. One is a logger, has been his whole life, and is free to express his desires to see the university obtain more lands so that they can develop the resources on them and explore that purpose, and does not seem to express any sentiment towards conservation or preservation of the land, which disturbs me.

So, hearing those types of statements coming from one of our regents, it seems to me that certain actions need to be taken to make sure that the land is going to be protected, and by stipulating limitations on any Federal transfer that is one way I see a possibility of doing that.

The CHAIRMAN. You are familiar with what funds the State budget in the State of Alaska?

Mr. TRITT. Budgets to the university?

The CHAIRMAN. The State budget, of course, which the university receives a significant amount of; where that comes from primarily?

Mr. TRITT. Yes. Oil revenue.

The CHAIRMAN. Do you know how much, approximately?

Mr. TRITT. To the university or to the State?

The CHAIRMAN. To the State.

Mr. TRITT. I could not say.

The CHAIRMAN. About 83 percent.

Mr. TRITT. Okay.

The CHAIRMAN. So you know, as we look at resources and the contribution of resources—and I assume we all accept our State dividend. That comes from resource development.

I noted in your testimony quite a criticism on logging on private land that you had some experience with. That was Native land?

Mr. TRITT. Correct?

The CHAIRMAN. Are you aware of who has the responsibility for maintaining the forest practices on private land?

Mr. TRITT. I believe that is the State.

The CHAIRMAN. And the State certainly has the obligation to properly manage that land, and if it is not managed correctly, why, the State should certainly take steps to ensure that it meets forest quality standards, because we have the opportunity with the Forest Service commitment to manage Federal lands, and I think it is fair to say that the Forest Service manages them in a professional manner relative to appropriate laws and forest stewardship. So if the State is inconsistent—and I think Mr. Powell perhaps can give us a little comparison.

Professionally, how do you see the State's management of its private lands relative to the Forest Service?

Mr. POWELL. I think in comparison, Mr. Chairman, the Forest Service has more rigid standards and guidelines. Overall, I think the State does a pretty good job within the limits of their staffing of trying to comply with the State laws. But they are very short of staffing and I am sure there are some situations where they are not at the standards that we would like to see.

But in comparison, the Federal standards are tighter and I think are more consistently applied.

The CHAIRMAN. Even though, it is kind of interesting, some of the increased Federal standards came from State standards.

Mr. POWELL. Well, I am not sure I would characterize it that way.

The CHAIRMAN. No, but I said some, which kind of indicates some of the—I think the buffer zones were first established under State authority and then expanded under Federal forests. So the State has provided, I think, a reasonable amount of leadership, and there are inconsistencies in State enforcement just as there are in Federal enforcement.

There is a myth associated with clear-cuts, and I noted a criticism of clear-cuts. Of course, clear-cuts are a reality. They occur in various forests for specific reasons. One can fly over the Cascades, a combination of national forests, a combination of private forests, and see extensive clear-cuts. Southeastern Alaska, the economics and the Forest Service dictate that that is the way timber sales are put up.

Unfortunately, there is a presumption brought on by the environmental community that, while these are certainly ugly, they are somehow the worst type of forest management practice. Mr. Powell, would you care to comment on the aspects of clear-cut as promoting second growth and bringing along a rejuvenation as compared to the other alternative of selectively logging and the damage that is done under that?

Mr. POWELL. Sure. I think you have appropriately characterized the controversy around clear-cutting, and that is not just in Alaska. That is a nationwide controversy. And there are many different opinions, but from a professional forestry standpoint there are certain tree species, some situations, and certain areas where clear-cutting is the appropriate silvicultural tool to use.

We use it in southeastern Alaska along with other types of harvest techniques. We have been very pleased with the regeneration of trees, as you have talked about. It is very successful in that.

There are other areas of controversy in terms of size and how you do it, how it is applied on the ground. So it is not appropriate everywhere, but we have been very successful in our use of it.

The CHAIRMAN. Have you put up any significant sales where you called for selective logging of just old growth, higher quality?

Mr. POWELL. We have.

The CHAIRMAN. And how does that work?

Mr. Powell: Most of those sales are younger sales. Some of those, in fact, have some active research in it at this time. We believe it will work. There are economic considerations when you do that.

The CHAIRMAN. How do you log it?

Mr. POWELL. A lot of that is done by helicopter.

The CHAIRMAN. So it has to have a price structure that would support the higher costs.

Mr. POWELL. Well, all of it is not done by helicopter.

The CHAIRMAN. Oh, no, just the higher grade.

Mr. POWELL. On some of our steeper ground, helicopters are used.

The CHAIRMAN. If you put up a sale and you simply high-grade it, then what happens? Are you subject to more blowdown of the remaining timber? It is less attractive, I assume, from the standpoint of anybody purchasing it if the high grade is gone.

Mr. POWELL. The concern we have as foresters again is to try and leave a forest that is productive for the future and to ensure that we leave trees genetically that are sound. But, not to characterize it as high-grading, we can have a selective harvest in the Tongass and we will have in the future, and there is some of that on private land as well. So it is one of the tools. It is just not a tool that works everywhere.

The CHAIRMAN. Well, I think, unfortunately, there is a mentality out there, fostered by the environmental community, clear-cuts are unacceptable.

Mr. KOEHLER. Senator, could I comment?

The CHAIRMAN. Sure.

Mr. KOEHLER. A couple things. The notion that, the myth that you talk about. I think certainly clear-cutting is a reality in southeastern Alaska and there are certain places that are going to get clear-cut and there are some places where SEACC has accepted that. What I would say is the problem of clear-cutting, as Brad Powell has noted, is usually the location and the size, and there are times it should not happen. There are many places that have been clear-cut that were critical winter range for deer and there is a serious problem when you remove all the forest.

The CHAIRMAN. Well, Mr. Koehler, you and I have been over this time and time again, and with the policies that are maintained, with adequate fringe areas around the beaches——

Mr. KOEHLER. This is not the hearing for that discussion, Senator.

The CHAIRMAN. It is quite evident that the State Department of Fish and Game that controls the harvest of deer takes into consideration the habitat. It is rather interesting that environmental groups never bring up the predator as a factor in the decline of the deer population. It is always the timber industry. And as one who looks at Kyuyu Island, where there is an overpopulation of deer or, excuse me, an overpopulation of wolves, there is virtually no deer hunting. When you look at Admiralty, Berenof, Chichagof, which have no wolves, lots of deer.

So I think it is interesting to bring up the other side of the issue, Mr. Koehler.

Mr. KOEHLER. There are also no wolves on those islands because there are no wolves on those islands; there never have been. Grizzly bears, by legend anyway, keep those wolves away.

The CHAIRMAN. That is right. It is too far for the wolves to swim.

Mr. KOEHLER. Yes, well, that is part of it.

The CHAIRMAN. That is the reason.

Mr. KOEHLER. But the other part of it is on Kyuyu there has been heavy logging on the north end, and the removal of habitat is a serious concern when you get into this predator-prey relationship.

The CHAIRMAN. So your contention is that the decline in deer on Kyuyu is due to logging rather than wolves?

Mr. KOEHLER. No, I would say there has been some wolf predation on Kyuyu. I think on Price of Wales Island there is——

The CHAIRMAN. Tremendous wolf predation.

Mr. KOEHLER. Senator, on Prince of Wales Island there is a very serious concern over the level of logging there and the impact it is having on wolves.

The CHAIRMAN. On wolves or deer?

Mr. KOEHLER. On wolves and in fact on deer. The habitat is a real problem. There is a serious concern about a whole collapse.

The CHAIRMAN. Well, as you and I both know, because we are familiar with it——

Mr. KOEHLER. We do not agree on this, obviously.

The CHAIRMAN. You have watched the deer totally disappear from Waranofsky Island, totally, as a consequence of a pack of wolves. You have seen what they have done on Edleton Island.

Mr. KOEHLER. Waranofsky is a tiny little island, Senator.

The CHAIRMAN. That is right, but it is habitat.

Mr. KOEHLER. Sure.

The CHAIRMAN. I mean, if it is a tiny little island and it has got an eagle's nest on it, look out; it becomes a very significant tiny little island.

45-544 98 - 3

But you have cyclical wolves, cyclical deer, and the point is clear-cuts are a reality. Clear-cuts make in the forest second growth process a realism that we have seen. I am sure, Mr. Powell, you have been down to Edna Bay, you have seen the second growth occurring down there, and I think you would agree that the greatest contribution the Forest Service could make to the second growth is a more aggressive thinning program to ensure that that healthy timber that is growing has a chance to expand its growth more dramatically.

Mr. POWELL. Just to comment on that, we certainly agree we need to thin many of those second growth stands, not only for timber production values but for wildlife values and others as well.

The CHAIRMAN. Well, my purpose in extending this discussion on clear-cuts is to simply point out and recognize that clear-cuts are a reality, clear-cuts have an application in the forest regrowth, and if there are poor logging practices they should be subject to appropriate authority to eliminate those.

Mr. Koehler, you oppose this land transfer in its broadest sense, is that correct?

Mr. KOEHLER. Yes, sir.

The CHAIRMAN. What do you think the university ought to do, just depend on the State for its entire funding? You know what the University of Washington does. They have the Olympic Plaza, a significant area in downtown Seattle that generates a tremendous amount of revenues, and the university can count on that for its maintenance and various other things. And of course, we are subjected to a situation where our university has to increase its tuition, had has to defer maintenance, because they have no long-term funding mechanism.

As the State addresses its responsibility to the university, the funds come from resource development. So what difference does it make to the environmental community and SEACC whether the State is proceeding with resource development to fund the university or the university as an agency or an arm of the State has some flexibility to address its needs through something that other universities have traditionally benefited from. Gee, our universities in the southwest have over a million acres.

What is the difference? Do you not trust the board of regents? You trust the legislature more?

Mr. KOEHLER. I certainly do not trust our State legislature very much, Senator, given their behavior over the last few years. And I think Mr. Tritt has commented on his lack of confidence in certain members of the board of regents. He did mention——

The CHAIRMAN. You might as well take on the delegation, you know, as far as confidence. We have differences of opinion, okay. That is what makes a melting pot, just like your contribution.

Mr. KOEHLER. We would certainly recognize that there is a very vocal member of the board of regents who certainly does not agree with SEACC on many things, but he gets a lot of play in the papers, including one that he owns.

However, I would say that the State has much more—State lands development restrictions are more restrictive than if the university managed the same lands, if the lands were transferred from the State to the university. I think that is one reason why the Governor has vetoed past legislation to make large transfers.

Our main concern here is that we believe that the university has been treated fairly. We believe the State has been given a generous statehood grant that consolidated the university grants, as Mr. Fry pointed out earlier, and we have very, very serious concerns about allowing national forest lands to be selected by the university, or anyone else for that matter, and other public lands as well. We do not think the case has been made.

I think it is interesting to note, I was up in Fairbanks recently. You mentioned, Dr. Komisar mentioned, the vital research role that the university is playing. There is a big Arctic research center being built up in Fairbanks right now that I believe is—I do not remember the cost of it. It is in the tens of millions of dollars. And a large percentage of the cost of that building is being paid for by the Japanese government.

I think that is an interesting situation. I do not know if that is the answer to the question. I do not think it is. But I think that, to go back to the State legislature, the legislature has been cutting the university budget repeatedly over the years and I think the State legislature should look more carefully at how they fund the university and do a better job.

The CHAIRMAN. Well, I do too. I assume if we had a representative of the State here, which unfortunately we do not, that the legislature would say: Well, we try to meet all our obligations as best we can, and there is never enough money to meet the requests of our constituents.

Dr. KOMISAR. Senator, could I make a brief comment about the board of regents?

The CHAIRMAN. Please proceed, Dr. Komisar.

Dr. KOMISAR. The board of regents is an exceptional group of Alaskans who are vitally interested in the university, but also vitally interested in the future of the State of Alaska. They are appointed for 8-year terms and, as you indicated, by the Governor, with the support of the legislature. Because of the 8-year terms, you have an overlap, a considerable overlap in terms of the political spectrum and the attitudes and feelings.

I think that the board of regents represents the full range of opinion in Alaska, and no single member of the board drives policy, but a majority of the board. Though we can all at times find ourselves disagreeing with a particular board member's position, I think the record of the board shows very sober consideration and very wise decisions.

The CHAIRMAN. I think the fact that there is disagreement among the board is healthy, just like there is disagreement here among the witnesses, whether it be Mr. Koehler or Mr. Fry or Mr. Powell.

I do not know who wrote the Governor's letter for him, but whoever did it did not do a very good job of research. I cannot help note a reference in the third paragraph where he says that he basically supports, what is it, S. 660. "However," he says, "it puts the Federal Government's hands on the steering wheel of the State decisionmaking process."

Can anybody enlighten me as to what that interpretation is? Because my understanding of this is this is a proposal for 250,000 acres of Federal land to go to the university, and the additional 250,000 acres that would come would be matching, only initiated if the State chooses to match.

So Mr. Fry, can you enlighten me as to how the interpretation that the Federal Government is on the steering wheel? If the State does not want to match the second 250, there is not 250 coming. And you are against it anyway.

Mr. FRY. I would hesitate to guess.

The CHAIRMAN. Well, maybe the press can enlighten me or maybe the Governor's office can. I am sure I will get a response.

Furthermore, in the letter with regard to Federal lands it says here: "The bill specifically identifies transfer of the National Petroleum Reserve (NPRA) and the Tongass National Forest lands." Is there any identification in the bill of those areas? There is not. There is no mention of them. So I find that somewhat disturbing, and would suggest that whoever wrote the letter for the Governor do a little better job of research.

A couple of other things. There is a couple of land exchanges before us, Mr. Koehler, that I am sure you are interested in. One is Hoonah and the other is Kake.

Mr. KOEHLER. Hoonah?

The CHAIRMAN. Hoonah and Kake, yes.

Mr. KOEHLER. I am not familiar with the Hoonah one. There is the Hood Bay land exchange that is going on over on the House side.

The CHAIRMAN. Yes, that is a third one.

But do you know whether you are supportive of the Hoonah or the Kake exchanges?

Mr. KOEHLER. Senator, I am honestly not familiar with the Hoonah exchange.

The CHAIRMAN. Well, as I understand them, the motivation is protection of their watersheds.

Mr. KOEHLER. I think the only one I am familiar with in that case is the Kake, the Gunnuk Creek exchange, and our board of directors has been supportive of that in general because we think that watershed is important to the community of Kake and some solution should be arrived at.

The CHAIRMAN. Well, the interesting thing, though—and that is where the parallel here is—is that these exchanges are certainly meritorious. I happen to support them. But the exchanges themselves give them an opportunity for a selection of land in the Tongass that would be used for resource development. You and I both know that.

Mr. KOEHLER. But they are very carefully selected, small acreages, and value for value exchanges.

The CHAIRMAN. They are selected for—just a minute. Let us be honest with one another. They are very carefully selected to select the very best timber that they can find, adjacent as much as they can to their existing area of road extension and so forth, so they can generate revenue.

Now, they are protecting the watershed. I am all for that. But I just want to point out the reality.

Mr. KOEHLER. They are also trading out of land they already own, Senator.

The CHAIRMAN. Sure.

Mr. KOEHLER. Rather than selecting new lands from the public domain.

The CHAIRMAN. That is correct.

Mr. KOEHLER. It is a different situation.

The CHAIRMAN. No, they are saying they do not want to cut their own lands. They want to save them for their watershed, and they are trading those for other lands.

Mr. KOEHLER. We would rather have them do a conservation easement on Gunnuk Creek if it would come to that. They say they will not do that. I do not think you can make the case that Gunnuk Creek is the same as grabbing 250,000 acres, Senator.

The CHAIRMAN. I think it is interesting to point out that there is an inconsistency here relative to this process.

Mr. KOEHLER. You cannot make that case, Senator.

The CHAIRMAN. Sure I can. I just made it.

Mr. KOEHLER. Go ahead.

The CHAIRMAN. And whether you agree with it or not is your own business.

Mr. KOEHLER. We do not agree with that.

The CHAIRMAN. But what I find kind of interesting is in the package of testimony you provided, you provided resolutions from both those areas.

Mr. KOEHLER. That is right.

The CHAIRMAN. In opposition to this.

Mr. KOEHLER. Right.

The CHAIRMAN. Yet those communities expect us to support their land exchange. So I am sending a little message out there that I hope will be reflected on by those communities.

Mr. KOEHLER. Your threats are so noted, but I think they do not like to see——

The CHAIRMAN. It is not a threat. It is a point that I think deserves consideration in conformity. And I do not expect you to agree.

Mr. KOEHLER. Thank you.

The CHAIRMAN. So we will leave it at that.

Incidentally, Mr. Koehler, I want to compliment you on the rather thorough job that you and your associates have done on the material you submitted, particularly the record of the delegation relative to your record, and your success rate has exceeded ours dramatically, which I commend you and those that carry your banner, relative to the number of issues that we have discussed and debated over the years.

But we are both getting up in the morning and starting again.

Mr. KOEHLER. Thank you, Senator.

The CHAIRMAN. That is I think what makes life interesting, and hopefully we can both respond to our constituencies as they would anticipate, with some degree of success.

I do not know. It seemed to me there were a couple of more things here.

Bumpers is a new grandfather this morning, so that disrupted a portion of the day.

Is there anything that anybody would like to say, because I apologize for my four votes that I had?

Mr. Fry.

Mr. FRY. No, thank you.

The CHAIRMAN. You are going to send a message back to the administration?

Mr. FRY. Loud and clear.

The CHAIRMAN. And Mr. Powell, you are still going to put up clear-cuts?

Mr. POWELL. We are going to put up a variety of timber sales on the Tongass, and we are looking forward to implementing the new Tongass plan and achieving those goals.

The CHAIRMAN. Well, we talked about that yesterday.

Mr. POWELL. We have talked about that not only yesterday, but a few times.

The CHAIRMAN. Yes. And we are going to take a good long look at your budget figures and your administrative costs, so you can expect to hear from us very soon.

Mr. POWELL. We look forward to working with you on that.

The CHAIRMAN. Mr. Koehler, your next role is what?

Mr. KOEHLER. I do not know. We keep throwing ourselves in front of whatever trains you send at us, Senator. I hope it slows down a little bit.

The CHAIRMAN. Oh no, we will have something else for you.

And Dr. Komisar?

Dr. KOMISAR. The university appreciates all your good efforts on our behalf.

The CHAIRMAN. Mr. Tritt.

Mr. TRITT. I concur with that, and I just would like to say, if the board of regents—if you are planning on encouraging the board of regents to look at this and propose some possible changes, I think there is a workable solution to this situation that most at this table could agree with eventually if people would just sit down and talk it out.

The CHAIRMAN. You see, my observation of the world from where I sit as an elected representative is that the people can do a much better job than we can do dictating from Washington and enforcing through Federal officials who—you know, the last witness we had from the U.S. Fish and Wildlife Service had never been to King Cove, had no appreciation for what it means. You have been out in the wilderness.

Mr. TRITT. I lived in Cordova.

The CHAIRMAN. Here is a community, you know, that only needs 7 miles across a wilderness to have some security for the people that live there so they can get out in an emergency. Eleven people have been killed trying to fly that short route, which is only about 18 air miles, and all they are asking for is 6 miles of road so they can get out.

And we are told by the Department of the Interior: You do not need R.S. 2477; all you need is a good case. Well, we are telling the Department of the Interior we think this is a good case. And here again—Mr. Fry, it is not your watch—the Department of the Interior comes up precommitted with a veto threat.

My answer to that is, let them threaten to veto if that is the response they are going to make. We will take them on, and hopefully we will be able to prevail on the merits.

But enough of that futuristic thinking. I hope that we can accommodate the university because, left to its own accord, the university will not have this opportunity again. This opportunity is here as a consequence of a commitment of the delegation and the recognition by the board of regents that the university needs to have some long-term funding mechanism. Whether it ever goes beyond the initial 250,000 acres that is in this bill, into the option of 250,000 from the State and a further 250,000 from the Federal Government, will depend of course upon the State.

But I very much want to and intend to pursue this, and I think that we can expect the board of regents to honor the confidence that has been placed in them by the Governor selecting them, whether it be the current Governor or a former Governor, and certainly the president of the university acting with the board of regents, with the student body, in ensuring that whatever selections are made and the disposition of those selections are done in a prudent manner, because we all have a responsibility to the environment and the ecology. Where we may have differences, we have a lot more science, a lot more knowledge than we ever had before on how to do things correctly.

So I wish you well, gentlemen. I thank you for your attendance at the hearing. I am sorry again for the interruption, but that is the way it goes around here.

Thanks very much. I wish you all a good day.

[Whereupon, at 11:49 a.m., the hearing was adjourned.]

APPENDIX

Additional Material Submitted for the Record

Statement of John Schoen, Executive Director, National Audubon Society

Mr. Chairman, we appreciate the opportunity to provide you with our views on S. 1092, the King Cove Health and Safety Act of 1997. We appreciate the Committee's interest in addressing safety issues affecting King Cove and Cold Bay, Alaska. The mission of the National Audubon Society, representing more than 550,000 Americans nationwide, is to conserve and restore natural ecosystems, focusing on birds, other wildlife, and their habitats for the benefit of humanity and the earth's biological diversity.

REFUGE BACKGROUND

Izembek National Wildlife Refuge was established in 1960, and in 1980 the Alaska National Interest Lands Conservation Act (ANILCA) designated the majority of Izembek NWR as wilderness. The refuge's management purposes include conservation of fish and wildlife populations and their habitats, as well as ensuring to the maximum extent possible, maintaining water quality and quantity within the refuge.

Izembek NWR and Wilderness is a critical stop-over site for many waterfowl. The entire population of the Pacific black brant uses the refuge as a staging area every fall. A number of other waterfowl use the refuge, including the world's population of emperor geese; the tundra swan, the only non-migratory swan population in the United States; and Steller's eider, a threatened species.

Kinzarof Isthmus is the linkage between the northern and southern ends of the Southwest Alaska Peninsula. The southern Alaska Peninsula caribou herd and Izembek refuge's high concentration of brown bear normally migrate across the Kinzarof Isthmus.

A number of salmonids and marine mammals are found in, and adjacent to, the refuge's waters as well. Sockeye salmon migrate through to spawning grounds. Harbor seals are found on and around the refuge's shoreline.

ACTION PROPOSED BY S. 1092

S. 1092 would authorize construction of a 30-mile road from King Cove, Alaska across the Kinzarof Isthmus, to Cold Bay, Alaska. The road would cross through the Izembek National Wildlife Refuge and Izembek Wilderness.

The bill further proposes a land exchange granting the right-of-way over Izembek NWR to the Aleutians East Borough. The King Cove Corporation would then grant land along the mouth of Kinzarof Lagoon to the U.S. Fish and Wildlife Service.

STIPULATIONS AND WAIVERS INCLUDED IN S. 1092

The bill enumerates three specific waivers to existing federal law. Section 22(g) of the Alaska Native Claims Settlement Act would be waived. That section insists that refuge lands continue to be subject to the laws and regulations governing use and development of the specific refuge, following conveyance to a native corporation. All but one section of title XI of the Alaska National Interests Lands Conservation Act (ANILCA) would be waived. By exempting the majority of title XI, the President would not be able to approve or disapprove of the application for a transportation or utility system through a wilderness area. The ANILCA title XI waiver would also exempt the road from requirements that the Department of the Interior continue to manage the wilderness area in the interests of the refuge and wilderness area. A third provision, section 707 of ANILCA, would be waived. This provision says the Secretary of the Interior may only approve a transportation system across refuge lands if there is no other alternative means of transportation available, and that the road would have to be planned to minimize harm to the refuge.

All provisions of the Wilderness Act regarding roadless areas applicable to Izembek NWR and Wilderness are modified by title XI of ANILCA. However, the ANILCA title XI waiver included in this bill eliminates nearly all of these protections and regulations. The road would also be free from National Environmental Protection Act (NEPA) requirements for the preparation of an Environmental Impact Statement (EIS). The bill states that the road would not significantly affect the human environment, hence waiving NEPA requirements for an EIS. The bill also lifts any requirements for consultation with the National Historic Preservation Act, although there are three known archeological sites within the vicinity of the road corridor. Finally, the bill violates provisions of the Federal Highway Act by granting the Aleutians East Borough rights to construct, operate and maintain electrical, telephone, or other utility facilities and structures within the right-of-way. The United States reserves the right to issue additional grants.

NEGATIVE EFFECTS ASSOCIATED WITH S. 1092

The environmental costs of constructing a road through this important wildlife habitat is likely to be significant. The proposed road would pass through the refuge's wilderness and bisect the narrow Kinzarof Isthmus. The resulting fragmentation of critical wildlife habitat will separate terrestrial populations of migratory and non-migratory mammals.

In addition, increased human access to this important waterfowl habitat will cause stress in bird populations, hindering their ability to store food energy for migration. Further access to this area would also result in an increase in human-caused mortality of bears. Although a legal sport harvest could be managed, it would be difficult to control illegal killing or defense of life and property killing.

The effects of a road across the Kinzarof Isthmus are also expected to increase silt-loads and decrease freshwater flowing into Kinzarof Lagoon. Decreased water quality could affect eelgrass growth which a number of fish, waterfowl and marine mammal species are dependent on.

Although the bill proposes a land exchange, the habitat offered is not of higher quality than the current refuge land, nor would it likely mitigate the losses of wildlife populations and diversity due to the construction, operation and maintenance of a road through the Izembek NWR and Wilderness. The U.S. Fish and Wildlife Service only enters into acre-for-acre land exchanges when the land the refuge receives has higher quality habitat than the land the refuge conveys to the other party. In this case, the refuge would give up very high quality habitat for habitat of lesser quality.

Additionally, the construction of a road through a wilderness area degrades the very wilderness qualities for which it was set aside.

AUDUBON'S OPINION

While we recognize the need for increased transportation safety between Cold Bay and King Cove, we do not believe this is an acceptable means to meet that goal. There are a variety of alternatives that address safety concerns that should be given due consideration before initiating such a project. These include the establishment of a small emergency response unit of the United States Coast Guard at Cold Bay airport with a helicopter and crew; the establishment of an all-weather port facility and marine ferry system between King Cove and Cold Bay; and improvement of the airport at King Cove.

We are also concerned about the three specific waivers to existing federal law enumerated in the bill, as well as the efforts to circumvent normal processes. The waivers suggest that community health and safety are not compatible with wildlife and habitat conservation. However, the alternatives listed above suggest that these priorities are not mutually exclusive. Unfortunately, the third waiver (Sec. 707, ANILCA) exempts the Department of the Interior from even exploring other alternatives.

For these reasons, we must oppose S. 1092. Thank you again for the opportunity to submit comments.

STATEMENT OF ALLEN E. SMITH, ALASKA REGIONAL DIRECTOR, THE WILDERNESS SOCIETY

Mr. Chairman, members of the committee, I am Allen E. Smith, Alaska Regional Director of The Wilderness Society. I live in Anchorage, Alaska. I submit the following testimony to the record on S. 1092, King Cove Health and Safety Act of 1997. I request that this testimony be printed in the written record of this hearing and request the opportunity to submit additional comments on S. 1092 to the record as appropriate.

Founded in 1935, The Wilderness Society is a non-profit membership organization devoted to preserving wilderness and wildlife, protecting America's prime forests, parks, rivers, deserts, and shorelands, and fostering an American land ethic. With 250,000 members nationwide, 1,200 of whom live in Alaska, The Wilderness Society and its members have had a long-standing involvement in the protection of the extraordinary wilderness and wildlife values of the national interest lands in Alaska, including Izembek National Wildlife Refuge and Wilderness.

SUMMARY STATEMENT

While The Wilderness Society fully supports improved transportation between King Cove and Cold Bay for safety and other reasons, we strongly oppose S. 1092 in its entirety and urge Congress to reject it. Without any reference to the fact in the text of the proposed bill, S. 1092 would remove and declassify a significant amount of a designated Wilderness Area of extraordinary international and national value to migratory wildlife species from the Izembek National Wildlife Refuge and Wilderness by land exchange in order to provide a right of way to build a road. Further, S. 1092 would bypass the Alaska National Interest Lands Conservation Act (ANILCA), the Wilderness Act, the National Environmental Policy Act (NEPA), and the Alaska Department of Transportation and Public Facilities (ADOTPF) Transportation Access Assessment now under way to assess needs and alternatives in order to make this decision.

S. 1092 CONFLICTS WITH THE PURPOSES OF IZEMBEK NATIONAL WILDLIFE REFUGE AND WLLDERNESS ESTABLISHED BY ANILCA AND PREEMPTS ALL GOVERNING FEDERAL ENVIRONMENTAL LAWS

Izembek National Wildlife Refuge was originally established in 1960 to protect its unique wildlife and habitat values. At the same time, the Alaska State Legislature established Izembek State Game Refuge to protect Izembek Lagoon. In 1980, Congress designated 95% of the 304,000-acre Izembek National Wildlife Refuge as Wilderness, to be free from roads and other development, and specified the following purposes for the refuge in Sec. 303(3) of ANILCA:

(i) to conserve fish and wildlife populations and habitats in their natural diversity including, but not limited to, waterfowl, shorebirds, and other migratory birds, brown bears, and salmonids;

(ii) to fulfill the international treaty obligations of the United States with respect to fish and wildlife and their habitats;

(iii) to provide, in a manner consistent with the purposes set forth in subparagraphs (i) and (ii), the opportunity for continued subsistence uses by local residents; and

(iv) to ensure, to the maximum extent practicable and in a manner consistent with the purposes set forth in subparagraph (i), water quality and necessary water quantity within the refuge.

The rich wildlife diversity and species abundance at Izembek has long been recognized internationally. In its *King Cove Road-Briefing Report* of August, 1997, (submitted to the record of this hearing) the U.S. Fish & Wildlife Service (USFWS) catalogued that species diversity and uses of the refuge for:

Pacific Brant—entire Pacific population uses refuge;
Emperor Geese—world's population uses refuge;
Steller's Eider—now listed as threatened under the Endangered Species Act, half of world population molt on refuge and 70% overwinter;
Tundra Swan—only non-migratory population in North America;
Brown Bear—highest densities on lower Alaska Peninsula;
Caribou—refuge is primary migration route and wintering area of southern Alaska Peninsula caribou herd;
Anadromous Fish—refuge has numerous small streams and coastal wetlands used by spawning fish that would be crossed by the proposed road; and
Wolf and Wolverine—road would access their habitats.

These are all sensitive species of wildlife that are easily disturbed and displaced by man's encroachment and require a wilderness habitat to protect them from such impacts. Such is the essence of why Izembek was established in 1960.

In designating Wilderness in 1980 on Izembek National Wildlife Refuge, Congress recognized and affirmed these protection needs by deciding there would be no roads or major development in the 95% of the refuge that it designated Wilderness. Wilderness is our nation's highest level of land protection, and is appropriate for the protection of this rich wildlife area.

In its Briefing Report, the USFWS concludes:

> The Service finds the road alternative contrary to the purposes of the refuge and foresees unacceptable environmental impacts if a road is constructed on refuge lands through the wilderness area.
>
> The Service supports further study and consideration of other alternatives, such as a marine link, which could provide increased safety, economic growth, and fewer ecological impacts.

The Wilderness Society concurs with the USFWS in these conclusions. A road through the Izembek National Wildlife Refuge Wilderness would destroy it and would encroach on the wildlife that use it. Such a road would clearly be incompatible with the Congressionally-mandated purposes for which the refuge was established.

Further, S. 1092 would bypass and preempt all federal laws and public processes that now govern and protect Izembek National Wildlife Refuge and Wilderness. S. 1092 preempts ANILCA, the Wilderness Act, NEPA, and the National Wildlife Refuge Administration Act.

Presented as a land exchange, S. 1092 fails to mention or even display the fact that it would declassify and exchange Wilderness lands out of the National Wilderness Preservation System (NWPS) established by Congress in the Wilderness Act in 1964, and clearly would set a dangerous precedent of compromising established units of the NWPS.

For all of these reasons, The Wilderness Society strongly opposes S. 1092.

S. 1092 CONFLICTS WITH AND PREEMPTS THE STATE OF ALASKA'S TRANSPORTATION ACCESS ASSESSMENT PLANNING EFFORT CURRENTLY REVIEWING KING COVE ACCESS PURPOSES AND NEEDS REQUIREMENTS

Alaska Department of Transportation and Public Facilities (ADOTPF) is currently studying the purposes and needs for transportation between King Cove and Cold Bay as part of its Alaska Peninsula Intermodal Transportation Project. ADOTPF has identified several alternative modes of transportation that it will review and evaluate for King Cove-Cold Bay after it has completed its purpose and needs assessment.

The alternatives will include at least:

1. No action, status quo use of aircraft and private boats;
2. New ferry service connecting King Cove and Cold Bay, either directly or from a new dock in Lenard Harbor to Cold Bay;
3. A road between the two villages across the Izembek National Wildlife Refuge Wilderness;
4. A road from King Cove to a new airport north of Mt. Dutton;
5. Hovercraft service between the two villages; and
6. An emergency Medivac helicopter.

The Wilderness Society could support some form of ferry service to connect King Cove and Cold Bay and we believe that the ADOTPF needs assessment will show that it is economically feasible as indicated by earlier studies by ADOTPF in 1994. The Wilderness Society has previously stated its support for improved access to King Cove via some form of ferry and we will continue to support efforts to provide such service. There are viable alternatives for access that do not require compromising Izembek National Wildlife Refuge Wilderness.

S. 1092 would preempt the results of the State of Alaska's transportation planning process to determine purposes, needs and alternatives and it would superimpose a road alternative on the refuge that would destroy the Wilderness character and wildlife values of the refuge.

For all of these reasons, The Wilderness Society strongly opposes S. 1092.

CONCLUSION

The Wilderness Society believes that the residents of King Cove and Cold Bay should have safe transportation between their villages, but we also believe that there are appropriate and safe alternatives that can be found without building a road through the Izembek National Wildlife Refuge Wilderness. The Transportation Access Assessment process now underway by the State of Alaska should be used to determine the needs and viable alternatives, not S. 1092.

Further, The Wilderness Society strongly believes that Izembek National Wildlife Refuge Wilderness is of inestimable value protected as it is, should be left in Wilderness without roads, and that Congress should not be drawn into compromising a significant unit of the National Wilderness Preservation System. ANILCA, the Wilderness Act, and NEPA should never be compromised or bypassed in considering potential impacts to such significant wilderness and wildlife values as exist there.

For these reasons, The Wilderness Society strongly opposes S. 1092 and urges Congress to reject it.

We thank the committee for this opportunity to submit testimony on S. 1092 and these important issues of the Izembek National Wildlife Refuge and Wilderness.

Statement of Jim Adams, Counsel, National Wildlife Federation, Alaska Office

The National Wildlife Federation (NWF) appreciates the opportunity to submit comments for the record on S. 1092, the King Cove Health and Safety Act of 1997. NWF, the nation's largest member-supported conservation education and advocacy organization, unites people from all walks of life in a common sense approach to protecting nature, wildlife and the world we share. While NWF fully supports improved transportation between King Cove and Cold Bay for economic and safety reasons, NWF opposes S. 1092 in its entirety. The proposed bill prematurely dictates an environmentally destructive "solution" to King Cove's transportation needs before the state of Alaska has defined those needs and determined the best method of addressing them.

REFUGE BACKGROUND

Izembek National Wildlife Refuge (NWR) was established in 1960. In 1980, the Alaska National Interest Lands Conservation Act (ANILCA) designated the majority of the refuge as wilderness. Wilderness is the nation's highest designation of land protection, and was created to ensure that increasing population, expanding settlement, and increasing mechanization do not occupy all areas in the United States. Instead, designated lands are places where the earth and its community of life remain "untrammelled by man." 16 U.S.C. § 1131.

The Izembek Lagoon and Wildlife Refuge was the first wetlands site in the United States to be recognized for its global importance by being placed on the List of Wetlands of International Importance. It is essential to a vast array of migratory waterfowl and shorebirds. Over 70% of Steller's eiders—added to the United States Fish and Wildlife Service's threatened species list just this year—overwinter at Izembek, and at various times it hosts the world's entire population of Pacific black brant and emperor geese.

The wilderness is as essential to mammals as it is to birds. The Joshua Green watershed is a key brown bear natal area for the Alaska peninsula. Denning density for portions of the wilderness average 7.3 bears per square mile. The wilderness also supports the Alaska Peninsula caribou herd, wolves, wolverines, and foxes.

THE BILL

S. 1092 would authorize the construction of a 30-mile road from King Cove to Cold Bay, Alaska. It would bisect a narrow 3-mile isthmus between Izembek and Kinzarof Lagoons—the favored habitat of most of the bird population in the area, and the spring and fall migration route for the Alaska Peninsula caribou herd.

The bill also proposes a land exchange granting a right-of-way over the refuge and wilderness to the Aleutians East Borough in exchange for land along the mouth of the Kinzarof Lagoon. The land the American people would receive in exchange for the road corridor is lesser quality habitat that would not mitigate the effects of the road corridor.

Finally, the bill would exempt the proposed road from most environmental protections and reviews. By declaring that the road would not significantly affect the human environment, the bill would exempt the road from NEPA review. Section 22(g) of the Alaska Native Claims Settlement Act—requiring that refuge lands transferred to native corporations continue to be subject to laws concerning development in the refuge—would be waived, as would all but one section of title XI of ANILCA. This would deny the President the opportunity to approve or disapprove the road, exempt the road from requirements that the Department of the Interior continue to manage the wilderness area in the interest of the refuge and wilderness, and exempt the road from requirements that it be planned to minimize harm to the environment, and be built only if alternatives did not exist.

THE ENVIRONMENTAL EFFECTS

The proposed road is likely to have significant disruptive environmental effects on the internationally recognized Izembek wetlands. Increased access to the area af-

45-544 98 - 4

forded by the road will stress bird and bear populations, both through hunting and increased human disturbances that drive species from prime habitat. The road will also result in the fragmentation of habitat for the bears, the caribou who migrate through the isthmus, and the many other species that utilize the isthmus. Finally, the road will decrease water quality in the area, ultimately leading to a degradation of the eelgrass in Kinzarof Lagoon upon which much of the ecosystem depends.

Apart from its impacts to the biological characteristics of the refuge, the road will destroy the wilderness character of the area it passes through. Put simply, a wilderness with a road through its heart is no longer a wilderness.

ALASKA'S PLANNING PROCESS

The state of Alaska is currently engaged in an analysis of the need for a road or another transportation alternative between King Cove and Cold Bay. A preliminary study suggested that a ferry between the two towns would meet the transportation needs of the area at a fraction of the monetary and ecological costs of the proposed road. Remaining safety issues could be addressed by the placement of a medical clinic in King Cove, or by the establishment of a small emergency response unit of the U.S. Coast Guard at Cold Bay airport with a helicopter and crew. Given that Alaska itself has not determined whether a road is necessary, a bill authorizing the road is premature.

CONCLUSION

Ultimately, this bill is a return to the bad old days of development without thought or planning. The state of Alaska is working hard, with the cooperation of NWF and other environmental groups, to determine King Cove's needs and to choose the transportation alternative that best meets those needs and the needs of the environment. It would be premature for Congress to dictate the choice of alternative, and irresponsible to exempt that alternative from most environmental review.

The National Wildlife Federation strongly opposes S. 1092. Thank you for the opportunity to comment.

STATEMENT OF CONSTANCE E. HUNT, DIRECTOR, FRESHWATER ECOSYSTEMS CONSERVATION, WORLD WILDLIFE FUND

World Wildlife Fund appreciates the opportunity to submit testimony on S. 1092, the King Cove Health ad Safety Act of 1997, on behalf of its 1.2 million members in the United States. This legislation would authorize the construction of a road from King Cove to Cold Bay, Alaska. The road would traverse the Izembek National Wildlife Refuge ad Wilderness Area. While sympathetic to the need of residents of King Cove for safe and reliable transportation routes, WWF must oppose this legislation. Our opposition is based both on issues of process and on the potentially significant environmental impacts of the proposed bill.

WWF believes that S. 1092 represents extremely poor public policy at both the national and international levels. The bill would force a land exchange on the U.S. Fish and Wildlife Service, which has objected to the construction of the proposed road through the Izembek Refuge and Wilderness Areas on the basis of wildlife habitat fragmentation and water quality deterioration that render the road incompatible with the purposes for which the refuge was established. The bill would bypass an ongoing effort led by the State of Alaska to evaluate various alternatives to improve transportation between the two communities. The bill would violate the obligations of the United States under the Ramsar Convention to conserve the ecological character of wetlands of international importance. Most egregiously, the bill would exempt the road from the National Environmental Policy Act, the Alaska National Interest Lands Conservation Act, and any other law. WWF believes that this waiving of laws, international conventions, and democratic process in order to avoid the evaluation of alternatives to the proposed road would be an inappropriate example for the United States to set in a world that we are attempting to guide towards security, democracy, and environmental awareness.

In addition to the bad precedent this legislation sets, the bill would authorize a road that could have significant, adverse environmental impacts on an ecosystem of international importance.

PENINSULA AIRWAYS, INC.,
Anchorage, AK, November 14, 1995.

Hon. TED STEVENS,
Hart Office Bldg., Washington, DC.

DEAR TED: This letter is to voice my support for the proposed road project between Cold Bay and King Cove.

King Cove is one of the most difficult routes we serve; even though only 15 miles away from Cold Bay. Due to the terrain there will never be other than VFR, daylight-only aircraft operations possible, with better than average weather necessary.

There have been at least five major aircraft crashes in the King Cove area in the last dozen years, one of them a medivac flight in which four lives were lost.

I remember a number of years when the Christmas mail had to be carried by a Peter Pan tender when we could not fly for a week at a time.

While Penair is the only scheduled carrier for King Cove, the revenue derived from that route is a small fraction of our overall income. I actually see an increase in our business because of the activities generated by such a road.

Apparently, the next step is to authorize a land exchange between the King Cove Corporation and the U.S. Fish & Wildlife Service for an easement through the Izembek Refuge.

I would urge the Congressional delegation and Secretary of the Interior to expedite this exchange.

Very truly yours,

ORIN D. SEYBERT,
President.

King Cove, AK, August 4, 1997.

Hon. DON YOUNG,
Chairman, House Resources Committee, Washington, DC.

Hon. FRANK MURKOWSKI,
Chairman, Senate Energy Committee, Washington, DC.

Hon. GEORGE MILLER,
Ranking Officer, House Resources Committee, Washington, DC.

Hon. DALE BUMPERS,
Ranking Member, Senate Energy Committee, Washington, DC.

I am writing in regard to the proposed road between King Cove and Cold Bay.

I was born and raised in King Cove and lived here all my life. I am 65 years old and loved living here. I am proud of the changes I have seen in our town. It is a much better place to live. When I grew up, we had kerosene lamps and had to pack water from the well or creek, chop wood and had outhouses. We appreciate the help we received from the different State and Federal agencies to receive the electricity, sewer and water, road, airfield, schools and boat harbor. I thank those of you that helped us over the years receive these funds to help better our community.

I believe we sincerely need a road to Cold Bay. The travel safety factor would be highly increased in many ways in regard to travel between the two communities.

The Fish and Wildlife people are dead set against a road on account of the ducks and geese. This doesn't make sense to me. Everyone that wants to hunt goes to Cold Bay by boat in the fall and travel through the lagoons with small skiffs and outboards and this has not impacted the birds. I cannot see where a road is going to have an effect on the eelgrass that they are so concerned about.

The emergency aspect is of utmost importance, trying to get to or from Cold Bay by plane is impossible 50% of the time due to extreme weather in the winter. At various times of the year, this percent is higher. High winds, snow flurries, fog, the flight between the communities encompasses very mountainous terrain. In the summer months, fog is a main factor. Since 1980, I have kept records of our travels to and from Anchorage and 50% of the time we had to travel by boat because of bad weather. My wife broke her arm and leg in 1985 and she had to wait here in King Cove in pain two days before a plane could pick her up to take her to Cold Bay. This was at a time when travel by boat was impossible. Our school children have been experiencing some very bad trips between here and Cold Bay on their sporting trips to other communities.

At this time, I am asking for your support for getting a road to Cold Bay. This is the only way we are guaranteed to get there. There are many times that even a boat cannot get to Cold Bay.

Thank you.

Sincerely,

RICHARD MACK.

King Cove, AK, August 28, 1997.

TO WHOM IT MAY CONCERN: This letter is in regard to the road to Cold Bay. We sincerely believe that this road is a necessity. My daughter, Sarina, who is now 11 years old, had to be medivaced to Cold Bay on a 86'-foot crab boat. At this time, Carol had gone into premature labor at 7 months. At about 9:30 pm., we had to get to Cold Bay. The weather was snowing, blowing and we got Carol on the boat with medical provider, Al Hall. On the 2½ hr. boat ride, Gayla Mareen. Carol went into serious labor and Sarina was delivered on the galley table of the boat.

We had to make our own incubator out of an electric heater and foil wrap. Sarina at this time weighed 2 lbs., 3 oz. At the dock in Cold Bay, another crew member on the boat and myself, lifted Carol on a stretcher, 30 feet up and during that time, her I.V. and arm got caught on the dock and we had to lower her back down and do this again.

After this, we got them out on Peninsula Airways, two engine Navajo, to Anchorage, where Sarina weighed one pound less. We are lucky that both Carol and our daughter survived this incident. Many women and babies can potentially go through this trauma. We feel it is not necessary and WE NEED THE ROAD TO COLD BAY.

Thank you for your consideration.

NICK BEAR.

King Cove, AK, August 29, 1997.

My name is Edwin Bendixen, I am 68 years old and have been a resident of King Cove for all of those years. I would like to address the Road from King Cove to Cold Bay. In all my years here, I have seen people die because there was no way for them to get to Cold Bay for medical purposes. In 1955, or there about, Cold Bay froze so that there was no way to get to Cold Bay. The only type of aircraft at that time was a grumman goose which was unable to land because of cold temperatures.

Now that we have a airport, the problem still remains. Weather is the major factor and at times a boat cannot get to Cold Bay for days.

I have lived and trapped on the Izembek Bay for 12 years and I know people from Cold Bay drive over a large portion of the refuge where the proposed road would go. If all the people in Cold Bay and transient hunters do not impact the wildlife, I cannot see where a road would.

I do not know who was responsible for the brief that was written for Fish & Wildlife in regard to the road. However, the report is not true entirely. They state that Kinzarof Lagoon would provide the "Only significant' eelgrass beds on the Pacific side of the Alaska Peninsula. They failed to mention Big Lagoon, Middle Lagoon, Little Lagoon, which are by far larger eelgrass beds than Kenzarof Lagoon. There are also a number of other places on the south side with eelgrass beds that ducks and geese feed on.

I have walked from Cold Bay to King Cove many times and I disagree immensely with the eelgrass statement. I strongly believe a road is needed between King Cove and Cold Bay. I know in the years ahead it will save many lives when people are unable to fly out of King Cove. We have lost enough people over the years trying to get out for medical reasons and in this day and age it should not continue.

I appreciate the time that you have taken to read my letter and hope you will take it into consideration in any decisions made in regard to this road.

Thank you.

Sincerely,

EDWIN BENDIXEN.

King Cove, AK, August 20, 1997.

TO WHOM IT MAY CONCERN: My name is Tatiana Bendixen. I am 65 years old, and I have lived in King Cove for 42 years. I have many times experienced the hazardous travel arrangements to Cold Bay, Ak for my own medical problems either by plane or boat. Many times I get seasick traveling by boat to Cold Bay which aggravates my medical conditions more. The dock conditions at Cold Bay in bad weather are treacherous to say the least. Trying to get off the boat when the boat rises in high winds, rain or snow is extremely hazardous. There are times that people have crawled across top houses of the boat on a plank over to the dock.

There are times that we cannot get to Cold Bay by plane or boat for days at a time. People have had to be lifted by ropes up to the dock or a make-shift sling. This only raises the risk of adding to the medical condition or the risk of getting killed in the process.

The road to Cold Bay is a necessity, and we cannot continue to go against fate with our own lives because of these conditions.

The people are aware of the Izembek and Kinzarof Lagoon wildlife. We have never abused our wildlife because it is also our subsistence and enhances our livelihood.

People that are against this road should come out and take the boat ride and see for themselves what we are up against before they make statements that are not true. We live in an environment that changes. Sometimes, we can go into four seasons within a few hours.

Thank you for your consideration.

Sincerely,

TATIANA BENDIXEN.

King Cove, AK, August 28, 1997.

TO WHOM IT MAY CONCERN: This letter is in regard to the road to Cold Bay from King Cove. My name is Tatiana Samuelson. I am 52 years old and have lived in King Cove all of my life. I would like you to take into consideration the seriousness of the need for a road to Cold Bay.

My husband, Walter Samuelson, Sr., had a major heart attack on February 1, 1989. At that time, we could not get him out of King Cove for two days because the weather was bad, no plane or boat was able to get to Cold Bay. Walter died at the age of 60 on February 1, 1992. My family believes that had Walter been able to get out of King Cove and to a medical facility sooner, he would not have had the major complications that lead to a heart transplant. Walter spent much of the four years in and out of hospitals. We went to Salt Lake City for the heart transplant.

We have lost many people in our community due to increased health complications by not being able to get to Cold Bay. We feel strongly that we need the road. We ask that you take this into serious consideration in any decisions in regard to the road to Cold Bay. We have a right to survival also.

Thank you.

TATIANA SAMUELSON.

EASTERN ALEUTIAN TRIBES, INC.,
Sand Point, AK, September 4, 1997.

Hon. DON YOUNG,
Chairman, House Resources Committee, Washington, DC.

Hon. FRANK MURKOWSKI,
Chairman, Senate Energy Committee, Washington, DC.

Hon. GEORGE MILLER,
Ranking Officer, House Resources Committee, Washington, DC.

Hon. DALE BUMPERS,
Ranking Member, Senate Energy Committee, Washington, DC.

DEAR SIRS: I am writing to express the deep concern that Eastern Aleutian Tribes (EAT) holds for the proposed Cold Bay/King Cove road project.

As I'm sure you've heard from others, the lack of a road connection between the communities creates problems when one considers the nature of the terrain, the frequent fogs and high winds that make flying dangerous at best and often impossible.

Cold Bay, with its long paved runway, serves as the jump-off point for all flights to and from Anchorage. As the regions health care provider, we are especially sensitive to this fact because we are frequently unable to medivac seriously or critically ill patients to the Alaska Native Medical Center in Anchorage for treatment.

In fact, the Cold Bay clinic was named in honor of Anna Livingston, a Community Health Aide from King Cove who was killed attempting to medivac a patient by air in bad weather.

Our health care providers are unanimous in the opinion that the road is a necessity for public safety. The location of the two communities is nearly unique in the Aleutian Islands, since there is a contiguous land route between them. Virtually every other community in the Aleutians is located by itself on an island and there is no option to join them in this way.

Construction of the road will halt the dangerous flight between King Cove and Cold Bay during medivacs, when the lives of all aboard are at stake, not only the life of the patient for whom the flight is being made.

I will be pleased to answer any questions you might have or to provide additional information on request.

Sincerely,

STEVE LEVINSON,
Executive Administrator.

[The following petition in support of an easement for a road to Cold Bay from King Cove was received with approximately 525 signatures:]

We, the undersigned, are residents, fishermen, seasonal workers, traveling public of King Cove and strongly support legislation that enables us to get access through the Izembek Refuge for a road to Cold Bay. We have, for many years, put up with the trauma of not being able to get to Cold Bay due to extreme weather or fog. We have had losses of family members, friends because of plane crashes, increased medical complications due to not being able to get to Cold Bay and the majority of the time this flight between King Cove is not safe due to bad weather. Cold Bay has the third largest airport in the State of Alaska.

KING COVE CORPORATION
P.O. Box 38 King Cove, Alaska 99612 497-2312

August 27, 1997

The Honorable Don Young
Chairman
House Resources Committee
Washington, DC 20510

The Honorable George Miller
Ranking Officer
House Resources Committee
Washington DC 20510

The Honorable Frank Murkowski
Chairman
Senate Energy Committee
Washington, DC 20510

The Honorable Dale Bumpers
Ranking Member
Senate Energy Committee
Washington DC 20510

This letter is in reference to The Road to Cold Bay from King Cove. The King Cove Corporation has offered a number of times, a land trade for easements through the Izembek Refuge for a road to Cold Bay. We have met with Fish and Wildlife this Spring to discuss this issue and feel they believe that the issue of a more safe mode of travel is real and of necessity to our community.

We have stated that there are no alternatives but a road to Cold Bay. The major issue being weather. There are too many times, when a plane cannot fly that a boat cannot get to the dock at Cold Bay. People in this community have for many years put up with the increased trauma of traveling to Cold Bay by boat when they have to leave for emergency medical reasons. There are some older residents who travel even in fair weather and still the weather in LEONARDS Harbor is turbulent and they do not like it. Some people take medication before they travel this flight to try to stay calm. Our community has grown over the years and the necessity to travel between these communities has increased.

The King Cove Corporation has agreed to give title to lands in the refuge to Fish and Wildlife for an easement through the refuge so that we can have a road. We are willing to work with Fish & Wildlife in regard to a road. Our office and staff has put circulated a petition in regard to the road and you can see that the community was fairly represented. We ask that you take into consideration the need for a safer mode of travel. Cold Bay has the third largest airport in the State of Alaska. We would like access to that airport for the people in this community for better health care that can be provided in Anchorage which is 500 miles away.

Thank you for your consideration.

Sincerely,

Dean Gould,
President

KING COVE CORPORATION
P.O. Box 38 King Cove, Alaska 99612 497-2312

August 28, 1997

The Honorable Don Young
Chairman
House Resources Committee
Washington, DC 20510

The Honorable George Miller
Ranking Officer
House Resources Committee
Washington DC 20510

The Honorable Frank Murkowski
Chairman
Senate Energy Committee
Washington, DC 20510

The Honorable Dale Bumpers
Ranking Member
Senate Energy Committee
Washington DC 20510

This letter is in reference to The Road to Cold Bay from King Cove. I have been the Vice-President of the King Cove Corporation for 10 past years and have met with Fish & Wildlife a couple of times in regard to a road both in Anchorage and in King Cove. We have proposed a land swap two times since I have been the Vice-President and there was a feasibility study done on this as early as 1986. I strongly disagree with Fish & Wildlife in regard to their assumption that people will take advantage of the wildlife in the Izembek Refuge and Kinzaroff Lagoon if there is a road. People have been hunting and fishing and trapping in this area for years, since the early 1900's that we are aware of and possibly earlier. Today people continue to take their boats in this area to hunt and fish. The people understand the importance of controlling their resources to not over hunt or fish. As it stands, many people from Cold Bay and transient hunters use the existing roads in the refuge. All users have not impacted any wildlife in the refuge.

Daniel Jerry, Fish & Wildlife, Anchorage, in one of our meetings out right stated that the only way we can get access through the refuge is through Congressional action. At this time, that is where we stand and hope you will take into careful consideration the importance of this issue to the people in the community of King Cove. People for many years have put up with continued hardships traveling between both communities. We have lost people in plane crashes, the delay in trying to get people out of King Cove has increased the medical problem, people have died because of this. We do not believe in this day and age we should continue to put up with this trauma and hardship.

Thank you for your consideration.

Sincerely,

Kenneth Mack,
Vice-President

ALEUTIANS EAST BOROUGH SCHOOL DISTRICT

P.O. Box 429
Sand Point, Alaska 99661-0429
Phone: (907) 383-5222
FAX (907) 383-3496

October 26, 1995

Senator Frank Murkowski
706 Hart Building
Washington, D.C. 20510-0202

Dear Senator Murkowski,

The proposed legislation authorizing a land exchange between King Cove Corporation and the U.S. Fish & Wildlife Service for an easement through the Izembek Refuge has our full support.

The easement would permit construction of a road from King Cove to Cold Bay, a town with a runway used by Boeing 727's of Reeve Aleutian Airways. Currently, residents of King Cove have to fly from a gravel strip between the peaks of the mountainous terrain surrounding on three sides. The gravel runway is often unusable due to turbulent, blustery winds rolling off the ridge lines. School functions are often delayed or canceled as a result.

As I write this letter, I am waiting in Cold Bay for winds to drop down at King Cove's runway enough to let us fly there with a consultant to train staff in newly adopted instructional materials. This type of turbulence delay is so common that schools from around the Aleutians rarely agree to home-home athletic agreements because the games historically have been too often canceled, and teams have been too often weather bound. I believe that many parents would happily permit students to travel down the proposed road during wind conditions when flying travel out of the current King Cove runway would have intimidated them, and prevented the activity.

The proposed 30 mile road would permit lower cost interaction of students and staff from Cold Bay School with students and staff at King Cove, and could enable future secondary programs serving both communities. King Cove students would have inexpensive access to the instructional advantages of the Izembek Refuge, as well as reduces expenses for Close-Up educational travel to the nation's capital and to Alaska's capital in Juneau. The activities program costs for the school district would be reduced. This may help us to sustain quality programs at a time when revenue increases are not keeping up with increasing costs.

We urge you to support the King Cove-Cold Bay road project by approving the land exchange legislation between U.S. Fish & Wildlife Service and King Cove Corporation. Thank you for your attention to this infrastructure need.

Sincerely,

Tom Ryan

Tom Ryan, Superintendent

cc: Bob Juettner, AEB Administrator
~~Board Members, AEBSD~~

SERVING

AKUTAN	COLD BAY	FALSE PASS	KING COVE	NELSON LAGOON	SAND POINT
Box 25	Box 128	Box 30	Box 6	Box 9	Box 269
Akutan, AK 99553	Cold Bay, AK 99571	False Pass, AK 99583	King Cove, AK 99612	Nelson Lagoon, AK 99571-9008	Sand Point, AK 99661
(907) 698-2205	(907) 532-2409	(907) 548-2224	(907) 497-2354	(907) 989-2225	(907) 383-2393

The Aleut Corporation

RESOLUTION 95-09

A RESOLUTION OF THE BOARD OF DIRECTORS OF THE ALEUT CORPORATION SUPPORTING THE KING COVE CORPORATION'S LAND TRADE FOR A ROAD EASEMENT THROUGH THE IZEMBEK NATIONAL WILDLIFE REFUGE.

WHEREAS, the community of King Cove is an isolated Aleut community located on the Alaska Peninsula and subject to severe weather conditions throughout the year; and

WHEREAS, medical emergencies are common during periods of bad weather: and

WHEREAS, the State of Alaska airport in Cold Bay provides the only viable means of medivacing people to Anchorage but it is often unreachable from King Cove which is a twelve-minute airplane ride away: and

WHEREAS, Governor Tony Knowles of Alaska has made the road from Cold Bay to King Cove one of his highest priorities; and

WHEREAS, the King Cove Corporation is willing to enter into a land exchange with the U.S. Fish & Wildlife Service to secure an easement through the Izembek National Wildlife Refuge; and

WHEREAS, Representative Young and Senators Murkowski and Stevens have agreed to sponsor the legislation necessary to make the land exchange a reality.

NOW, THEREFORE, BE IT RESOLVED that the Board of Directors of The Aleut Corporation support and endorse the land exchange between the King Cove Corporation and the Department of Interior for a road easement through the Izembek National Wildlife Refuge to link King Cove and Cold Bay.

PASSED AND APPROVED, the 12th day of October, 1995, at a duly called meeting of the Directors of The Aleut Corporation by a vote of 9 for and 0 opposing.

Alice Petrivelli, President

Attest:

David Nevzuroff
Assistant Secretary/Treasurer

Ref: J:\BOD\1995\0092

4000 Old Seward Hwy, Suite 300 Anchorage, Alaska 99503 (907) 561-4300 FAX (907) 563-4328

August 1, 1997

The Honorable Don Young
Chairman
House Resources Committee
Washington, D.C. 20510

The Honorable George Miller
Ranking Member
House Resources Committee
Washington, D.C. 20510

The Honorable Frank Murkowski
Chairman
Senate Energy Committee
Washington, D.C. 20510

The Honorable Dale Bumpers
Ranking Member
Senate Energy Committee
Washington D.C. 20510

Fr: Bonita Babcock
PO Box# 125
King Cove, Alaska 99612

Re: The proposed road between King Cove & Cold Bay

I was born and raised in King Cove, I have been a life long resident for 33 years. I am the mother of 3 children and am currently awaiting the birth of my 4th child. I have a deep appreciation and love for this community and its residents. In a place like this, it is not uncommon to know everyone in town, being that the population is not that large. On occasions when tragic events occur, it effects the whole community. It is especially devastating when deaths or extreme life threatening injuries occur and we are left with the knowledge, that if only there were a way to get the injured or dying person to Cold Bay, that a Life Flight could take them to a major hospital to save them. As I'm sure you're aware, near fatal accidents, heart attacks, pre-mature labor, and other life threatening incidents don't only happen when the weather is flyable or when a boat can make the trip over to Cold Bay. We desperately need a road to assure our access to emergency medical facilities.

A very dear Uncle of mine, died some years back, when his plane crashed into a mountain, due to wind and snow. He was a life long Alaskan, and an experienced bush pilot, but our weather is not always predictable. It wasn't long after he was killed , that I was trapped in a snow-storm, in a small plane. The pilot and I were flying in circles, in a valley between King Cove and Cold Bay. I was 8 months pregnant with my 3rd child. I was having complications with the pregnancy, due to diabetes and had to no alternative but to fly to Anchorage. A flight that normally should have taken 10 minutes, took 30 minutes. If it weren't for the knowledge of an experienced and level headed pilot, and plenty of prayer, I am sure my remains would be lost , somewhere on the side of one of the mountainous terrain that surround our beautiful community.

I work as an Emergency Dispatcher, and Police Clerk for the City of King Cove. Over the past 4 years at my job, I have seen many people transported from our community, in emergency situations by plane and boat . A lot of these transports would never have been nearly as traumatic for the accident victims and EMS personnel, if only our ambulance could have been driven to the Cold Bay airport .

Please consider our desperate need for this small stretch of road. It will be a tremendous step in improving the quality of life for the people that live this community.

Thank you for your time,

Bonita Babcock

Kathy Bear
PO Box 151
King Cove, Ak 99612

To Whom It May Concern:

I am writing in regards to getting a road to Cold Bay from King Cove. I am a medical provider in King Cove, CHA. Being a medical provider, I know how hard it is to get people out of our community for medical purposes, when we are unable to provide for them here.

Often when we have to medivac someone from out clinic to our nearest hospital, which is 500 miles away in Anchorage, we have to go by plane or boat to Cold Bay.

There have been a few times that I can recall when we've had to be sitting here at our clinic with a patient who needed to be further evaluated or needed more extensive medical care that we cannot provide for them here because we may not have the expertise or facilities.

We have had to keep patients that needed critical care because of the weather. When the weather is bad, and a plane or boat to Cold Bay, we do the best we can by taking turn with shifts at the clinic.

I also recall when the medical provider had to do a medivac and it was late at night, the plane crashed and never made it to Cold Bay, killing everyone on board. At that time, she was the only provider in the community and we had to go without one for many months. Had there been a road to Cold Bay, this would not have happened.

Out community has approximately 900 people. However, at peak times, Peter Pan Seafoods employs 200 to more 550 people. This does not count the fishermen who are here during the various fishing seasons. In an average month, we have had as many as 200 or more visits in the clinic in one month. Many times there is one medical emergency after another, one day to the next. We fly a medical provider with each medivac. There have been times, we have had only a skeleton crew here and have had to rely on the EMS squad. Sometimes, we travel to Cold Bay for medical emergencies there when there is no medical provider there. Each time, we do so, we put our lives and the lives of our patients at risk.

We appreciate you taking this into consideration and hope that we can get a road to Cold Bay.

Sincerely,

Kathleen Bear

Kathleen Bear, CHA

My name is Marilyn Mack. I am writing this letter of behalf of the King Cove Vol Rescue Squad. I have been involved with the rescue squad since 1981.

There have been a few times when I wished we had a road to Cold Bay. One time in particular comes to mind when we had a medical emergency with an older gentleman from peter pan. At the time the weather was to bad for flying, we considered taking him out by boat and remember discussing the situation with the nurse practicer and then deciding against the boat because of icy conditions at the time on the dock in Cold Bay. We kept the patient overnight in the clinic and took turns monitoring him throughout the night. The next day we were able to get him to Anchorage for further evaluation.

Another incident that had a big impact on us as a rescue squad is the time we had to monitor one of our squad members husband that was had a heart attack. We kept him in the clinic for 3 days while it was blowing up to 100mph during the entire time.

A number of years ago my friends brother died in a plane crash between Cold Bay and King Cove while trying to help a crew member that had lost his leg in an accident aboard a fishing vessel. I remember that a lot of the towns-people had to go to the airport and use their lights from there vehicles to light up the runway. Later at her home as we were all sitting around the living room my friend had a call come in on the radio which she answered.

someone wanted to know all the names of the people on the plane. She named off the people and we continued visiting. Later we would find out about the crash.

This is just some of the situations that have happened that have affected us deeply.

I am also very concerned as a parent of two teen-agers that play sports and have to travel on a road schedule. There have been times when I would not let our kids go on a sports trip because of the weather the planes fly in.

I too have to travel out of town for training to keep up my certification and it is very up setting when the weather is not good enough to fly but its still can be blowing, [illegible] foggy down to the ground, snowing so hard you can't see but they tell you it will clear once you take off.

I am very much in favor of a road to Cold Bay and hope you take our concerns very seriously.

respectfully Yours

Marilyn Mack
King Cove Vol Rescue Squad
P.O. Box 89
King Cove Ak 99612

LAW OFFICES
BIRCH, HORTON, BITTNER AND CHEROT
A PROFESSIONAL CORPORATION
1155 CONNECTICUT AVENUE, N.W. . SUITE 1200 . WASHINGTON, D.C. 20036-4308 . TELEPHONE (202) 659-5800 . FACSIMILE (202) 659-1027

[illegible]

October 7, 1997

The Honorable Frank H. Murkowski
Chairman, Committee on Energy
and Natural Resources
United States Senate
322 Hart Senate Office Building
Washington, D.C. 20510

Jo,
Please include
660
Hearing
Record

Re: S. 660

Dear Mr. Chairman:

Enclosed for sumission to the Committee's hearing record on S. 660 is an addendum to the prepared Testimony of Dr. Jerome B. Komisar, President of the University of Alaska.

Please contact this office if you have any questions.

Sincerely,

BIRCH, HORTON, BITTNER
AND CHEROT

William P. Horn

Enclosure

cc: Dr. Jerome Komisar
James Parrish
Martin Epstein

F:\801754\8\JAP2054

ADDENDUM TO TESTIMONY OF DR. JEROME B. KOMISAR

BACKGROUND AND HISTORY OF SECTION 906(b) OF THE ALASKA NATIONAL INTEREST LANDS AND CONSERVATION ACT

Section 906(b) of the Alaska National Interest Lands Conservation Act (ANILCA) granted the State the right to select an additional 75,000 acres "In full and final settlement of any and all claims by the State of Alaska arising under the Act of March 4, 1915 (38 Stat. 1214) [*the Alaska School Lands Act*], as confirmed and transferred in section 6(k) of the Alaska Statehood Act,". The provision further provides that through exercise of the selection rights the State, "... shall be deemed to have relinquished all claims to any right, title or interest to *any school lands* [emphasis added]..." which failed to vest under either statute, including unsurveyed lands.

Section 906(b) was enacted to address a very specific inequity affecting the State of Alaska's <u>school lands</u> and was not intended to, nor does it, resolve or effect the University and its claims under the 1915 Alaska School Lands Act. In fact, its existence demonstrates that Congress has previously recognized that the provisions of the Statehood Act, particularly Section 6, did not permanently resolve and eliminate the United States' obligations under the 1915 Act.

<u>The Alaska School Lands Act</u>

The 1915 Alaska School Lands Act did three things. First, it reserved each section 16 and section 36 in every township in Alaska for, "the support of common schools in the Territory of Alaska;...." Second, it reserved each section 33 in each township in the Tanana Valley for support of what became the University of Alaska. Both of these reservations were conditioned upon the lands first being surveyed by the United States. Third, it dedicated several sections and partial sections outside of Fairbanks as a campus site for the University.

It is by now well-known that the University never received most of the lands reserved to it by the 1915 Act because of the failure of the federal government to survey most of Alaska by the time the Statehood Act was passed. The Territory, likewise, did not receive many of the school lands reserved for it for the same reason. However, Alaska also experienced another obstacle which was more familiar.

It was not unusual in Alaska and other western states to find that by the time public lands were surveyed, those sections 16 and 36 which had been reserved for school lands had already been claimed by homesteaders. In 1891 Congress enacted R.S. 2275 (43 U.S. 851) to address this problem. In instances in which sections reserved for school lands have been previously settled, R.S. 2275 granted to the states the right to make in lieu selections of an equal amount of acreage. However, in its original form, it did not extend to the Territory of Alaska. Moreover, it dealt specifically and only with reservations of sections 16 and 36 and did not provide in lieu selections for sections 33 or other entitlements. 43 U.S. 851.

In 1979, when H.R. 39, the legislation that would eventually be enacted as ANILCA, was being considered, the State determined that approximately 75,000 of the acres that had been reserved as school lands had been claimed by homesteaders or otherwise made unavailable, most of it in the Anchorage area. Alaska, however, was never able to take advantage of the in lieu privileges which R.S. 2275 provided other states.

In 1958, Congress amended R.S. 2275 to broaden its applicability and this included clarifying its applicability it to Alaska. P.L. No. 85-771 (72 Stat. 928). It did so by amending the Alaska School Lands Act to incorporate by reference the in lieu selection provisions of R.S. 2275. 72 Stat. 929-30. This provision replaced an earlier proviso which attempted to extend the provisions of R.S. 2275 to Alaska. Thus, the in lieu provisions of R.S. 2275 were made applicable to Alaska only thru the Alaska School Lands Act.

Time, once again, was not on Alaska's side. P.L. No. 85-771 was signed into law on August 27, 1958. Unfortunately, the Statehood Act was signed on July 7, 1958, and became effective on January 3, 1959. Section 6 of the Statehood Act repealed the 1915 Alaska School Lands Act, including the in lieu selection provisions, thereby preventing Alaska from having the benefit of the provisions and selection lands in lieu of the approximately 75,000 acres which it had been denied.

It was this inequity, which involved the State's <u>school</u> <u>lands</u> only, that Section 906(b) was intended to remedy. That is why Congress granted the State the additional 75,000 acres. And that is why the statute makes specific reference to *school lands*, which is a statutory term of art which referred only to lands dedicated to support of a system of "common" schools in Alaska. The 1915 Alaska School Lands Act and statutes distinguished between *school lands* and University lands. Thus, it would have been inconsistent with prior legislation to suddenly include University lands within the meaning of *school lands*.

Discussions with individuals who represented the State on the matter confirm that it was never intended nor even contemplated that section 906(b) would also resolve the University's longstanding land claim. Thus, it is incorrect to conclude that Section 906(b) of ANILCA discharged the federal government's land obligations to the University.

Furthermore, the existence of Section 906(b) actually refutes the proposition put forth by the federal government that the conveyances under the Alaska Statehood Act had satisfied all of its land obligations in Alaska, including the University's entitlement. In fact, this provision convincingly demonstrates that Congress has previously concluded, apparently without objection from the executive branch, that the Statehood Act had <u>not</u> resolved all land obligations in Alaska.

ALASKA MINERS ASSOCIATION, INC.
501 W. Northern Lights Blvd., Suite 203, Anchorage, Alaska 99503 FAX (907) 275-7397 Telephone (907) 276-0347

September 5, 1997

Honorable Frank Murkowski
United States Senate
Washington, DC 20510

RE. S.660, University of Alaska Lands Act

Dear Senator Murkowski,

We are writing to urge passage of Senate Bill 660 which would allow the University of Alaska to select and receive title to various federal lands. As a land grant college the University of Alaska has not received a land base to support its programs and this Act will correct that situation.

It is important that the University be allowed to select lands from any of the remaining federal BLM and USFS lands not in a federal Conservation System Unit (CSU). Huge areas of Alaska have already been placed in CSU's and these areas are closed to all economic development. Much of the land having the highest potential for mineral development, or other economic opportunity, has already been placed in federal CSU's such as national parks, preserves, wildlife refuges, wilderness areas, etc. The University should therefore be allowed the widest possible selection rights from the National Petroleum Reserve-Alaska (NPRA), the Bureau of Land Management (BLM) and the U.S. Forest Service lands.

There are several important aspects in S.660 that we would underscore. The time limit of 48 months seems an appropriate time frame to allow selections to occur without causing an excessive length of uncertainty of land status. The provision whereby failure to act on a tentative selection by the Secretary of Interior will result in an automatic approval is also very important. It is also important that NEPA procedures will not be required.

There are some areas where we would suggest changes. First, we would recommend that the amount of land to be selected under phase one of the bill be increased from 250,000 acres to 500,000 acres. Given that so much of the most economically prospective lands in Alaska are already in CSU's, the remaining lands will likely be of lesser value and the University should be allowed to select a greater acreage.

Second, the limitation that selections should not exceed 275,000 acres needs to be clarified. It appears that the intent is that not more than 10% over-selection will be allowed and we concur. However, the argument could be made that after receiving title to 200,000 acres, the over-selection could still be 275,000 acres. This needs clarification.

Third, serious consideration should be given to not including all of the University inholdings in this bill The private land known as the Brady Glacier nickel deposit, for example, should be kept in University ownership. There are many development scenarios that would not adversely impact the surrounding CSU that must be evaluated before title to this area is lost The future and value to our nation are not served by locking up such a valuable mineral the deposit

We believe that this bill can be a win-win for the University, the State of Alaska, and the nation The funding of our educational system will be a near term beneficiary, both by virtue of revenue generation and through added educational opportunities created by ownership of the lands The State and Nation will benefit from added University funding and they will benefit when natural resources not now in production are developed providing jobs and economic activity that would not otherwise be created

Thank you for this opportunity to comment on this important piece of legislation If there is anything we can do to help insure its swift passage please contact me

Sincerely,

Steven C Borell, P E.
Executive Director

cc Senator Ted Stevens
Congressman Don Young
Governor Tony Knowles
President Jerome Komisar

Alaska Outdoor Council
Rod Arno, President
P.O. Box 2790
Palmer, Alaska 99645
Tel: (907) 376-2913
FAX (907) 376-7100

September 5, 1997

Ms. Deborah Williams
Special Assistant to the Secretary
U S. Department of the Interior
Anchorage, Alaska 99501
FAX 907-271-4102

Dear Ms. Williams,

The Alaska Outdoor Council would again like to express our thanks to the Department, the Secretary, and all appropriate staff for the strong opposition to the so-called "landless natives" issue at the recent Senate Natural Resources Committee hearing on S. 967. Further, we appreciate the strong statements, opposing the "University Lands Bill" (S.660), which could ultimately transfer up to five hundred thousand acres of the Tongass National Forest, and other areas, to the University of Alaska.

The Alaska Outdoor Council (AOC) is a coalition of over 45 Alaskan hunting, fishing, and outdoor clubs with memberships of over 10,000. Our organization is dedicated to defending Alaska's hunting and fishing heritage, ensuring conservation and advancing fair allocations of fish and wildlife resources. The AOC is also the official state association of the National Rifle Association.

The AOC strongly opposes unjustified attempts to appropriate some of the highest quality public lands on the Tongass National Forest Combined, S967 and S.660 would ultimately pull hundreds of thousands of acres of valuable lands out of the Tongass public land base and transfer them to private for profit interests. Those interest will of course move quickly to convert available timber and other resources into quick cash. These acres, once free and open public lands will be subject to scenarios where hunting, fishing, and recreational uses are encumbered or brought into conflict with private extractive operations.

The Department testimony before the Senate Natural Resources Committee on July 29, 1997 correctly opposed the Section 8 language of S. 967. That language would result in the unwarranted and improper transfer of public lands to groups which failed to meet the basic corporate requirements of the Alaska Native Settlement Act. The reopening of ANCSA to such unwarranted claims, will open the door to a substantial number of similar claims throughout Alaska.

Fish and Wildlife populations and public access have been adversely affected by private land ownership throughout the Southeastern Region. Remaining public lands must be safeguarded if we are to preserve the values for which Alaskans cherish this portion of the State. The Department of Interiors stand on these insupportable grabs for a public resources are appreciated and in the best interest of all Alaskans as well as the visiting public from all over the world. Thank you and keep up your good work on the Tongass National Forest.

Sincerely,

Rod Arno, President
Alaska Outdoor Council

cc: Senator Ted Stevens
Senator Frank Murkowski
Representative Don Young
Governor Tony Knowles
Senator Robin Taylor
Territorial Sportsmen, Inc.

STATEMENT OF

ALASKA STATE SENATE PRESIDENT MIKE MILLER

AND

ALASKA STATE HOUSE SPEAKER GAIL PHILLIPS

BEFORE THE

UNITED STATES SENATE

ENERGY AND NATURAL RESOURCES COMMITTEE

REGARDING

S. 660

UNIVERSITY OF ALASKA LANDS BILL

September 11, 1997

Mr. Chairman and members of the U.S. Senate Energy and Natural Resources Committee. We thank you for this opportunity to present this statement regarding S. 660, the proposed legislation to grant federal lands to the University of Alaska.

We are very pleased and encouraged to see this effort to redress the inequitable treatment which the University of Alaska received compared to other land grant colleges. With this legislation the University will finally receive an adequate and appropriate land base with which to support its role as the sole public institution of higher education in the State. This grant will benefit all future generations of University of Alaska students as well as the State's many resource-based industries bringing new jobs and increased economic activity.

There are several features of the bill that we wish to comment on specifically. First, we recommend that you seriously consider increasing the number of acres made available to the University under the primary federal grant. In Alaska, 250,000 acres is not a relatively large amount of land given, that with nearly 140 million acres already set aside in Park, Refuges and Wilderness areas, the University will have only a very restricted area of land available for selection.

It is important also that the State have input into the land selection and approval process. The bill does allow for public comment as part of the Secretary's review process. However, we believe the State should be provided with some specific notice of the University's selections and the Secretary's decision.

We recognize that there has been criticism of this bill in regard to the availability of land within the Tongass National Forest for selection. In response, we wish to point out that the University, which has shown itself to be a careful and rational manager of resources, would still be subject to significant regulatory oversight It would have to adhere to an array of state and federal conservation and environmental standards. Moreover, the bill contains adequate safeguards to ensure that the only lands which can be conveyed are those which can be developed without significant harm to any federally protected lands. The fact that the lands and resources will be of immeasurable impact to higher education is apparently unimportant to many critics. Alaska is simply seeking the same benefits which California, New York, Vermont and other states received many, many years ago. Clearly, some of those who raise these objections are, in fact, opposed to the University, or any entity other than the federal government, controlling public lands regardless of the need or the justification for doing so.

The benefits of this land grant cannot be understated. The University of Alaska is called upon to serve the entire State. Based simply on Alaska's size and geography, this is a challenge unknown to other state university systems. It is made even more challenging by the diverse nature of the communities and needs it serves. The State budget has many demands on it and one unfortunate, but realistic, result is that all of the University's programs and functions cannot receive complete funding. By finally completing its land base, the University will be in a position to govern and control its funding resources.

In closing, we wish to confirm our strong support for S. 660 and for the effort to finally provide the University of Alaska, and the many Alaskans it serves, its due entitlement.

TONY KNOWLES
GOVERNOR

STATE OF ALASKA
OFFICE OF THE GOVERNOR
JUNEAU

P.O. Box 110001
Juneau, Alaska 99811-0001
(907) 465-3500
Fax (907) 465-3532

September 8, 1997

The Honorable Frank Murkowski
United States Senator
706 Hart Building
Washington, DC 20510

Dear Senator Murkowski:

I appreciate the opportunity to comment on two Alaska-related bills your committee will be dealing with in an upcoming hearing.

S. 660, University of Alaska Land Grant

I support the responsible transfer of federal lands to the university. The university system is very important to Alaska and higher education is the backbone of the future of our economy. It is the state's understanding that the university, as a land grant institution, has received less acreage than almost any other similar college in the United States. In fact, only Delaware has obtained a smaller land grant from the federal government than the University of Alaska has received, and all land grant colleges in the western states of the United States have obtained substantially larger land grants than the University of Alaska.

Accordingly, the state supports a federal land grant to the university to make amends for the small initial federal grant. Your Senate Bill 660 provides for a total of 500,000 acres of federal land to be given to the university. I support this. However, S. 660 puts the federal government's hands on the steering wheel of the state decision making process by linking part of the federal grant to complementary state action. I urge you to eliminate this provision. Historically, the federal government has assumed the responsibility for providing acreage to land grant institutions and research conducted by the Alaska Department of Law into the legislative history of the Alaska Statehood Act does not reveal any Congressional view that federal lands previously provided to the university would be subject to conditions of state supplemented acreage.

Furthermore, the Alaska Statehood Act reflects a general policy that oil and gas lands shall remain in the general grant category for the benefit of all the people of Alaska. It is difficult, too, for us to evaluate fully the state match portion of this bill pending the final receipt by the state of the 15.5 million acres we have not yet received from the federal government under the Alaska Statehood grant.

Regarding federal lands, your bill specifically identifies transfer of National Petroleum Reserve-Alaska (NPR-A) and Tongass National Forest lands. I have consistently opposed the transfer of lands to the university from the NPR-A or the Tongass National Forest. It would be unwise to transfer substantial common property resources like NPR-A or the Tongass that are of great importance to all Alaskans to a single interest.

Additional conveyance of oil and gas interests to third parties will reduce state general fund revenues, and further fragment ownership in oil and gas prospective areas, thus potentially delaying leasing prospects.

The transfer of Tongass lands would throw more uncertainty into the Tongass for the timber industry and communities that have already felt a great deal of disruption and could adversely affect the U.S. Forest Service calculation of annual harvest levels under the Tongass Land Management Plan. Further, ten communities in Southeast Alaska have passed resolutions opposing the legislation because of the additional pressure for logging the bill would place on the Tongass, particularly LUD IIs designated by the Tongass Timber Reform Act.

Inclusion of the NPR-A and Tongass provisions will generate additional opposition from various interest groups and jeopardize any federal transfer to the university. Accordingly, I recommend deletion of this provision.

It is the state's hope that we can find ways to provide adequate funding for the University of Alaska, without dividing Alaskans. Accordingly, we appreciate that S. 660 provides for a notice in the Federal Register and for a public comment period. It is important that any transfer of lands should include an open public process which includes all interested groups to discuss specific lands to be conveyed.

S. 1092, King Cove to Cold Bay Road

The Alaska Department of Transportation and Public Facilities (DOT&PF) has initiated a study to establish the purpose and need to improve the transportation connection between the cities of King Cove and Cold Bay. The study includes an economic analysis which will be used to determine the level of need, as well as an assessment of health and safety issues. The study will identify a variety of aviation, highway, marine, or some combination of alternatives that could meet this need. In undertaking this study, we will consider community impacts, wildlife and environmental factors, fiscal implications, and the use of alternative communication technology, including telemedicine.

An initial series of meetings were held in the communities in early June to discuss the project and to begin to assess the need. An economic analysis has been ongoing with a draft report anticipated later this month. The DOT&PF has expanded its agency and public involvement efforts, including an on-site investigation by agency, conservation group, and DOT&PF personnel to King Cove and Cold Bay last week to visit potential locations for transportation facilities. This technical tour provided the participants a first-hand experience using the existing transportation facilities serving these communities. Participants discussed the whole range of identified issues facing this project, including health and safety, land status, environmental impacts, and the feasibility and potential locations of possible transportation solutions.

Public meetings will be held later this fall to discuss the findings of the economic analysis and the results of the technical tour study, and to gather additional information on existing conditions and traditional uses within the study. The final report defining the purpose and need of the project should be available in November. The state would be happy to share the report with the committee as soon as it is completed.

The findings of this report will determine if there is sufficient purpose and need for the state to proceed with a Preliminary Design and Environmental (PD&E) phase of project development. It is during the PD&E phase that the alternatives will be analyzed in detail and a preferred alternative will be selected as part of the study process for the project.

Thank you for allowing the State of Alaska to share its views with you.

Sincerely,

Tony Knowles
Governor

ALASKA STATE LEGISLATURE,
HOUSE OF REPRESENTATIVES,
Fairbanks, AK, September 3, 1997.

Hon. FRANK H. MURKOWSKI,
Senator, Hart Building, Washington, DC.

DEAR SENATOR MURKOWSKI: Thank you for filing Senate Bill 660: "To provide for the continuation of higher education through the conveyance of certain public lands in the State of Alaska to the University of Alaska."

We wish to be placed on record as supporting S. 660 and completing the land grant to the University of Alaska. We feel it will greatly assist the continuation of higher education in Alaska.

We believe it is appropriate to include the matching provisions in the bill. During this next legislative session, we are committed to working on legislation to provide the state match as required in section 6 of SB 660.

We look forward to working with you on our mutual goal of fulfilling the commitment to establish the University of Alaska as a land grant university.

Sincerely yours,

Representative Pete Kelly, Senator Gary Wilken, Senator Mike Miller, Representative John Davies, Representative Tom Brice, Representative Al Vezey, Representative Gene Therriault, Representative Jeannette James.

ARCTIC SLOPE REGIONAL CORP.,
Barrow, AK, September 11, 1997.

Hon. FRANK MURKOWSKI,
Chairman, Committee on Energy and Natural Resources, U.S. Senate, Dirksen Senate Office Building, Washington, DC.

Dear Senator Murkowski: On April 28, 1997, you introduced S. 660, a bill "[t]o provide for the continuation of higher education through the conveyance of certain public lands in the State of Alaska to the University of Alaska. . . ." Section 1 of the bill states that the purpose of this measure is to fulfill a commitment made by Congress to establish the University of Alaska as a land grant university "with holdings sufficient to facilitate operation and maintenance of a university system for the inhabitants of the State of Alaska." Pursuant to the terms of this bill, the University of Alaska is granted and entitled to select up to 250,000 acres of federal lands (or reserved interests in lands) in or adjacent to Alaska as a federal grant. In addition, the University is granted and entitled to select up to another 250,000 acres in federal lands, provided that any additional acres are granted on a matching acre-for-acre basis to the extent that the State of Alaska shall first grant to the University additional State-owned land in Alaska.

S. 660 is significantly different and more detailed than the provisions of S. 1851, a bill on the same subject you introduced in the last Congress on June 7, 1996.

1. BACKGROUND

A. The Iñupiat people and NPR-A

Arctic Slope Regional Corporation ("ASRC") was established under the terms of the Alaska Native Claims Settlement Act of 1971 ("ANCSA"). ASRC represents the interests of its 7,300 Iñupiat Eskimo shareholders and holds title to the Regional Corporation's land entitlement on Alaska's North Slope.

There are eight Iñupiat Eskimo Villages located on the 56 million acre North Slope. Four of these villages—Atqasuk, Barrow, Nuiqsut and Wainwright—are located within the 23.7-million-acre National Petroleum Reserve-Alaska ("NPR-A"). Two other villages—Anaktuvuk Pass and Point Lay—are located near NPR-A and the residents of these villages also use NPR-A lands and subsistence resources.

In 1971, the NPR-A was a "Naval Petroleum Reserve". Because of this area's status as a Naval Reserve, ASRC was permitted, under the terms of ANCSA, to acquire any lands within NPR-A's 23.7 million acres, including the subsurface estate beneath the four Eskimo Villages located within NPR-A. The village subsurface estate issue was addressed, in part, in 1980 by section 1431(o) of the Alaska National Interest Lands Conservation Act. Despite this fact, ASRC was still not permitted to select any of its general ANCSA land entitlement from any of the other NPR-A lands around the villages, from any of the lands on which ASRC's shareholder's cabins and hunting and fishing camp sites are located, or from any of the NPR-A subsurface estate which potentially contains oil, gas, and other mineral resources.

In addition to the long-standing injustice to the Iñupiat people imposed by the denial of an opportunity for ASRC, their Regional Corporation, to select lands within NPR-A, there has, in recent months, been another related development. This new development is the proposal now under review by the Department of the Interior ("DOI") and the Bureau of Land Management ("BLM") to conduct oil and gas lease sales in the northeast portion of NPR-A. An NPR-A lease sale in an area located near and heavily used by the residents of three of our villages—Barrow, Nuiqsut and Atqasuk—could further complicate and delay ASRC's efforts to secure a land base in NPR-A.

B. University of Alaska and NPR-A

It is ASRC's view that the University of Alaska would utilize its S. 660 land grant to select high value lands which have the capacity to generate revenue. This being the case, it is likely that the University would seek to make selections in areas of NPR-A which are prospective for oil and gas, because there are very few other land areas on the North Slope that are available for selection. Also, there has been an important new oil discovery at Alpine, an area near NPR-A's northeast border. The proposed oil and gas lease sale in the northeast area of NPR-A, an area that has generated significant oil industry interest. It is, therefore, ASRC's judgment that the University's primary area of interest for its land selections would be NPR-A and the Outer Continental Shelf areas adjacent to producing and prospective areas of the North Slope. As a result, ASRC has an obligation to insure that the provisions of S. 660 do not limit or unduly impinge on ASRC's and our Iñupiat shareholder's interests.

2. ASRC'S CONCERNS ABOUT SEVERAL OF THE PROVISIONS OF S. 660

ASRC has significant concerns with the policy approaches evident in a number of S. 660 provisions as introduced. These are discussed below.

A. S. 660 conflicts with ASRC's NPR-A land exchange objectives

ASRC has made several proposals to the Secretary of the Interior for land exchanges with the DOI on Alaska's North Slope. One of these proposals involves NPR-A lands and has been pending since 1994. If concluded, this exchange would permit ASRC to secure title to lands within NPR-A near the four villages, in important subsistence use areas, and in areas where ASRC shareholders have cabins and hunting and fishing camps. The land exchange that ASRC has proposed to DOI would expand the Gates of the Arctic National Park by adding to the Park 1.2 million acres of ASRC's private lands in the Killik River area. The National Park Service had identified these lands in the 1970's as a unique North Slope ecosystem, highly desirable as an addition to the Gates of the Arctic National Park. ASRC's land exchange proposal would advance national land use and conservation objectives and, at the same time, result in fair and equitable treatment to the Iñupiat people who live within or near NPR-A. The State of Alaska has also expressed interest in acquiring lands in NPR-A through a land exchange with DOI.

ASRC's major concern is that S. 660, in its present form, gives the University of Alaska the right to select lands within NPR-A and on the North Slope ahead of ASRC, the local Regional Native Corporation. The land grant and entitlement provided for in S. 660 would permit the University to select lands within NPR-A that ASRC has been and is seeking to acquire in its pending land exchanges with DOI. This means that ASRC's ability to select lands would be secondary to the University of Alaska. When the proposed lease sales being developed by DOI and BLM are factored in, it means that ASRC's land exchange proposal for NPR-A has now been bumped back to third choice behind the University and behind the DOI lease sale.

In short, the provisions of S. 660 would grant to the University of Alaska land selection rights in NPR-A which have been and are still being denied ASRC's shareholders, the Iñupiat people who are the historic residents of this area and the North Slope. This could lead to serious conflicts over important subsistence use areas, over lands on which cabins, hunting and fishing camps are located, and over other Iñupiat traditional land uses within NPR-A. To the extent the University of Alaska's land selections and entitlement under S. 660 are deployed to maximize revenue potential, a conflict could also arise with ASRC's objective of securing oil and gas and other mineral rights for its shareholders within NPR-A through land exchanges.

Clearly, before any action is taken on S. 660, amendments and procedures need to be developed which will fully recognize and protect the objectives and the interests of ASRC, its shareholders, and the six Iñupiat Villages located within and near NPR-A.

B. S. 660 conflicts with Iñupiat policy on OCS development

A second major concern relates to the provisions of S. 660 which authorize the University of Alaska to select lands on the Outer Continental Shelf ("OCS"). Section 2(a) and Section 6(a) grant and entitle the University of Alaska ". . . to take . . . federal lands (or reserved interests in lands) in or adjacent to Alaska as a federal grant." It is ASRC's understanding that the "or adjacent to Alaska" language constitutes an authorization for the University to select lands on the OCS.

The Alaska Eskimo Whaling Commission, the North Slope Borough and other groups representing the interests of the Iñupiat have long opposed and expressed serious reservations about OCS oil and gas development adjacent to the North Slope. The Iñupiat people are dependent upon the OCS and other marine areas for the important subsistence resources they contain.

The bowhead whale, seals, walrus, fish, and ducks, geese and other birds constitute a major portion of the Iñupiat diet. It is the position of the Iñupiat people that "onshore" areas of the North Slope should be developed for their oil and gas potential before any efforts are made to open "offshore" areas which are important nursery and habitat areas for bowhead whales, marine mammals, fish and other wildlife species. The Iñupiat people are confident about the safety of onshore oil and gas development after thirty years of experience. They have little confidence, however, that the oil industry has the technology or experience to safely produce oil and gas in the wind-driven, frigid, shifting ice packs in the long dark winters on the Arctic Ocean.

The Federal OCS leasing process provides numerous opportunities for public participation by local residents prior to decisions being made about a proposed lease sale. Through these public participation processes, the Iñupiat people have been able to educate and to inform decision-makers, thereby influencing those proposed leasing decisions which present extraordinary safety or environmental risks, or that threaten vital subsistence resources or marine habitat. At the same time, in areas where OCS leases have already been issued, the Federal permitting process provides opportunity for the Iñupiat people to be heard regarding how exploration and developmental activities are to be conducted. For example, conflicts between oil exploration and development on the OCS during the fall bowhead whale hunt by subsistence hunters from the Villages of Nuiqsut and Kaktovik have been addressed and resolved by agreements with the oil industry and Federal agencies.

The provisions of S. 660 authorize the University of Alaska to select prospective and valuable OCS lands adjacent to the North Slope. However, S. 660 does not contain any provisions to provide notice or other protection to the Iñupiat people who live on the North Slope. The University, in selecting and managing these fragile and important lands, would not be subject to any of the provisions now governing Federal oil and gas leases on the OCS under the terms of S. 660.

3. OTHER CONCERNS WITH THE PROVISIONS OF S. 660

A. Diminishment of ANCSA purposes and objectives

Section 2(b)(6)(B) of S. 660 establishes an exclusive standard under which the Secretary of the Interior may object to tentative selections of the University of Alaska. Under this provision, the Secretary may object ". . . if and only if he demonstrates that a conveyance of such to the University . . . (B) will have a significant adverse impact on fulfillment of the Alaska Statehood Act or the Alaska Native Claims Settlement Act. (43 U.S.C. 1601)."

ASRC's position is that, if a tentative land selection of the University of Alaska in any way impinges upon or prevents the accomplishment or the fulfillment of the Alaska Native Claims Settlement Act's provisions or purposes, or the legitimate land objectives of any Village or Regional Corporation, the Secretary's objection to that particular land selection of the University should not be limited or qualified in any way. Instead, the Secretary's objections should be heard and they should stand. The "significant adverse impact on fulfillment" standard for ANCSA's purposes and objectives is, in ASRC's judgment, improper and inappropriate.

B. Limitations on judicial review

The judicial review provisions of Section 5 of S. 660 should not operate only for the benefit of the University of Alaska. If other parties—the State of Alaska, ANCSA Corporations or other holders of lease or property interests in Alaska—are aggrieved by the decisions or actions of the Secretary under S. 660, they should have all of the same rights as the University of Alaska to seek judicial review and to proceed against the Secretary and the University.

4. CONCLUSION

In mid-August 1997, the University of Alaska's attorney and land management officer called upon ASRC officials in Anchorage to discuss S. 660 and ASRC's views on this measure. ASRC appreciates their recognition of our concerns and their willingness to discuss and address these concerns.

ASRC does not oppose the financial objectives the University of Alaska seeks to achieve. An economically strong and financially viable University system serves the best interests of all Alaska residents. Quality education is and should be one of the highest priorities of our State.

ASRC representatives are available to work with the University of Alaska, its representatives, the Chairman and members of this committee, the committee staff and other members of the Congressional delegation to develop amendments and legislative language which properly address the significant issues noted above.

I respectfully request that this letter be made a part of the hearing record and the committee's official files on S. 660.

Sincerely,

JACOB ADAMS,
President.

○